JUMP Math 3.1

Book 3 Part 1 of 2

W9-CHP-532

Contents

jump math

MULTIPLYING POTENTIAL.

JUMP Math
Toronto, Ontario
www.jumpmath.org

Writers: Dr. John Mighton, Dr. Sindi Sabourin, Dr. Anna Klebanov
Consultant: Jennifer Wyatt
Cover Design: Blakeley Words+Pictures
Special thanks to the design and layout team.
Cover Photograph: © iStockphoto.com/Michael Kemter

ISBN: 978-1-897120-68-2

Permission to reprint the following images is gratefully acknowledged: pp. 91 and 93: Coin designs © courtesy of the Royal Canadian Mint / Image des pièces © courtoisie de la Monnaie royale canadienne.

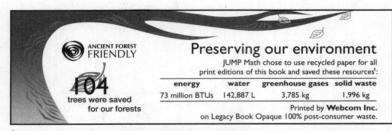

Preserving our environment

JUMP Math chose to use recycled paper for all print editions of this book and saved these resources[1]:

energy	water	greenhouse gases	solid waste
73 million BTUs	142,887 L	3,785 kg	1,996 kg

Printed by **Webcom Inc.**
on Legacy Book Opaque 100% post-consumer waste.

ANCIENT FOREST FRIENDLY

404 trees were saved for our forests

FSC
Recycled
Supporting responsible use of forest resources
Cert no. SW-COC-002358
www.fsc.org
© 1996 Forest Stewardship Council

[1]Estimates were made using the Environmental Defense Paper Calculator.

Printed and bound in Canada

A note to educators, parents, and everyone who believes that numeracy is as important as literacy for a fully functioning society

Welcome to JUMP Math

Entering the world of JUMP Math means believing that every child has the capacity to be fully numerate and to love math. Founder and mathematician John Mighton has used this premise to develop his innovative teaching method. The resulting materials isolate and describe concepts so clearly and incrementally that everyone can understand them.

JUMP Math is comprised of workbooks, teacher's guides, evaluation materials, outreach programs, tutoring support through schools and community organizations, and provincial curriculum correlations. All of this is presented on the JUMP Math website: **www.jumpmath.org**.

Teacher's guides are available on the website for free use. Read the introduction to the teacher's guides before you begin using these materials. This will ensure that you understand both the philosophy and the methodology of JUMP Math. The workbooks are designed for use by children, with adult guidance. Each child will have unique needs and it is important to provide the child with the appropriate support and encouragement as he or she works through the material.

Allow children to discover the concepts on the worksheets by themselves as much as possible. Mathematical discoveries can be made in small, incremental steps. The discovery of a new step is like untangling the parts of a puzzle. It is exciting and rewarding.

Children will need to answer the questions marked with a 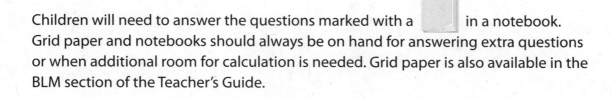 in a notebook. Grid paper and notebooks should always be on hand for answering extra questions or when additional room for calculation is needed. Grid paper is also available in the BLM section of the Teacher's Guide.

The ⬡ means "Stop! Assess understanding and explain new concepts before proceeding. "

Contents

PART 1
Patterns & Algebra

Number Sense

Measurement

Probability & Data Management

Geometry

PART 2
Patterns & Algebra

Number Sense

Measurement

Probability & Data Management

Geometry

Tom finds the **difference** between 9 and 6 by counting on his fingers. He says "6" with his fist closed, then counts to 9, raising one finger at a time.

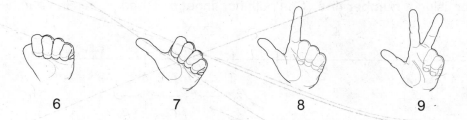

6   7   8   9

When he says "9", he has raised 3 fingers. So the difference or "gap" between 9 and 6 is 3.

- -

1. Count the gap between the numbers. Write your answer in the circle. (If you know your subtraction facts, you may find the answer without counting.)

a) 2 ② 4 ✓   b) 3 ② 5 ✓   c) 5 ③ 8 ✓   d) 6 ② 8 ✓

e) 4 ① 5 ✓   f) 3 ① 4 ✓   g) 4 ② 6 ✓   h) 7 ② 9 ✓

i) 2 ③ 5 ✓   j) 3 ③ 6 ✓   k) 1 ③ 4 ✓   l) 4 ③ 7 ✓

m) 5 ⑤ 10 ✓   n) 1 ⑤ 6 ✓   o) 5 ② 7 ✓   p) 2 ⑤ 7 ✓

q) 5 ④ 9 ✓   r) 3 ④ 7 ✓   s) 7 ③ 10 ✓   t) 6 ③ 9 ✓

BONUS

u) 19 ② 21 ✓   v) 8 ④ 12 ✓   w) 28 ④ 32 ✓   x) 17 ⑤ 22 ✓

y) 19 ③ 23 ✗ (4)   z) 46 ⑤ 51 ✓   aa) 37 ③ 40 ✓   bb) 99 ② 101 ✗

PA3-1: Counting (continued)

What number added to 6 gives 9?   6 + ? = 9

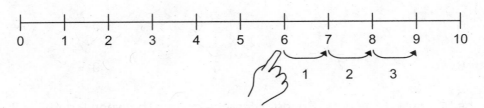

Anne finds the answer using a **number line**. She puts her finger on 6 and counts the number of spaces between 6 and 9.

She counts 3 spaces, so: 6 + 3 = 9

and: 9 is 3 **more than** 6

and: 3 is called the **difference** between 9 and 6

2. Use the following number line to find the <u>difference</u> between the two numbers. Write your answer in the box.

a) 3 + [2] = 5 ✓

b) 2 + [4] = 6 ✓

c) 4 + [3] = 7 ✓

d) 8 + [2] = 10 ✓

e) 7 + [5] = 12 ✓

f) 11 + [3] = 14 ✓

g) 10 + [2] = 12 ✓

h) 4 + [1] = 5 ✓

i) 12 + [3] = 15 ✓

j) 13 + [2] = 15 ✓

k) 2 + [6] = 8 ✓

l) 9 + [5] = 14 ✓

m) [2] + 12 = 14 ✓

n) 3 + [7] = 10 ✓

o) [3] + 8 = 11 ✓

BONUS

p) [9] + 3 = 12 ✓

q) 1 + [8] = 9 ✓

r) 2 + [10] = 12 ✓

s) [6] + 8 = 14 ✓

t) 4 + [7] = 11 ✓

u) 6 + [9] = 15 ✓

v) [9] + 6 = 15 ✓

w) [10] + 4 = 14 ✓

x) 3 + [12] = 15 ✓

3. Use the following number line to find the <u>difference</u> between the two numbers. Write your answer in the circle.

a) 12 ③ 15 ✓

b) 13 ④ 17 ✓

c) 11 ③ 14 ✓

d) 22 ② 24 ✓

e) 19 ④ 23 ✓

f) 17 ① 18 ✓

g) 14 ⑦ 21 ✓

h) 15 ④ 19 ✓

i) 16 ④ 20 ✓

j) 13 ⑥ 19 ✓

k) 11 ④ 15 ✓

l) 17 ⑦ 24 ✓

m) 13 ③ 16 ✓

n) 12 ⑤ 17 ✓

o) 21 ② 23 ✓

p) 18 ④ 22 ✓

q) 13 ⑩ 23 ✓

r) 14 ⑧ 22 ✓

s) 11 ⑧ 19 ✓

t) 12 ⑫ 24 ✓

4. Fill in the missing number.
   HINT: Use the number line to find the <u>difference</u> between the smaller and the larger number.

a) 15 is __2__ more than 13 ✓

b) 20 is __3__ more than 17 ✓

c) 23 is __7__ more than 16 ✓

d) 22 is __2__ more than 19 ✗ 3

e) 18 is __3__ more than 15 ✓

f) 16 is __1__ more than 15 ✓

g) 20 is __1__ more than 19 ✓

h) 17 is __4__ more than 13 ✓

i) 23 is __5__ more than 18

What number is 4 **more than** 8? (Or: What is 8 + 4?)

Carlo finds the answer by counting on his fingers. He says "8" with his fist closed, then counts up from 8 until he has raised 4 fingers.

| 8 | 9 | 10 | 11 | 12 |

The number 12 is 4 **more than** 8.

---

1. Add the number in the circle to the number beside it. Write your answer in the blank.

a) 3 ④ __7__ ✓   b) 9 ② 11 ✓   c) 6 ③ __9__ ✓   d) 4 ④ 8 ✓

e) 7 ⑤ 12 ✓   f) 6 ④ 10 ✓   g) 2 ⑧ 10 ✓   h) 9 ⑥ 15

i) 10 ⑧ 18 ✓   j) 17 ⑨ 26 ✓   k) 14 ⑦ 21 ✓   l) 12 ⑤ 17

BONUS

m) 27 ② 29 ✓   n) 35 ⑤ 40 ✓   o) 52 ③ 55 ✓   p) 47 ④ 51 ✓

q) 36 ⑥ 42 ✓   r) 82 ⑤ 87 ✓   s) 97 ④ 101 ✓   t) 95 ⑧ 103 ✓

2. Fill in the missing numbers.

a) __9__ is 3 more than 6   b) __9__ is 2 more than 7   c) __10__ is 4 more than 6

d) __9__ is 1 more than 8   e) __9__ is 5 more than 4   f) __17__ is 4 more than 13

g) __15__ is 6 more than 9   h) __14__ is 7 more than 7   i) __22__ is 5 more than 17

Tara wants to continue the number pattern.

6 , 8 , 10 , 12 , _?_   14

She finds the **difference** between the first two numbers by counting on her fingers.
She says "6" with her fist closed and counts until she reaches 8.

6   7   8

She has raised 2 fingers so the difference between 6 and 8 is 2.

②
6 , 8 , 10 , 12 , _?_   14

She checks that the difference between the other numbers is 2.

② ② ②
6 , 8 , 10 , 12 , _?_

To continue the pattern, Tara adds 2 to the last number in the sequence.
She says "12" with her fist closed and counts up until she has raised 2 fingers.

12   13   14

② ② ② ②
6 , 8 , 10 , 12 , _14_

----

1. Extend the following patterns.
    NOTE: It is important to start by finding the gap between the numbers.

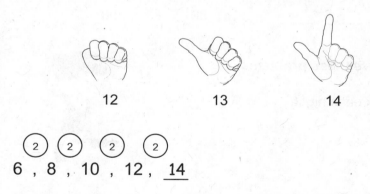

a) 1 ②, 3 ②, 5 ②, _7_, ② _9_, ② _11_   b) 0 ②, 2 ②, 4 ②, _6_, ② _8_, ② _10_

c) 2 ③, 5 ③, 8 ③, _11_, ③ _14_, ③ _17_   d) 0 ③, 3 ③, 6 ③, _9_, ③ _12_, ③ _15_

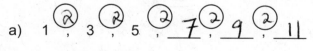

e) 0 , 5 , 10 , ___ , ___ , ___

f) 5 , 7 , 9 , ___ , ___ , ___

g) 3 , 7 , 11 , ___ , ___ , ___

h) 2 , 6 , 10 , ___ , ___ , ___

i) 4 , 8 , 12 , ___ , ___ , ___

j) 10 , 15 , 20 , ___ , ___ , ___

k) 1 , 4 , 7 , ___ , ___ , ___

l) 5 , 9 , 13 , ___ , ___ , ___

m) 11 , 13 , 15 , ___ , ___ , ___ , ___ , ___

BONUS

2. Extend the following patterns.

a) 1 , 6 , 11 , ___ , ___ , ___

b) 5 , 12 , 19 , ___ , ___ , ___

c) 21 , 24 , 27 , ___ , ___ , ___

d) 86 , 88 , 90 , ___ , ___ , ___

Use increasing sequences to solve these problems.

3. Mary reads 3 pages of her book each night.
    Last night she was on page 34.
    What page will she reach tonight?

4. Jane runs 10 blocks on Monday.
    Each day she runs 2 blocks further than the day before.
    How far does she run on Wednesday?

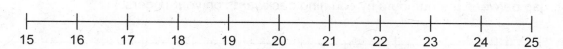

What number must you **subtract** from 22 to get 18?
Dana finds the answer by counting backwards on her fingers. She uses the number line to help.

22   21   20   19   18

Dana has raised 4 fingers. So 4 subtracted from 22 gives 18.

---

1. What number must you <u>subtract</u> from the bigger number to get the smaller number?

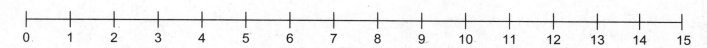

a) 7 (− 3) 4   b) 6 ◯ 3   c) 9 ◯ 7

d) 5 ◯ 1   e) 8 ◯ 4   f) 10 ◯ 5

g) 12 ◯ 9   h) 5 ◯ 4   i) 10 ◯ 4

j) 14 ◯ 9   k) 5 ◯ 2   l) 12 ◯ 4

m) 13 ◯ 9   n) 15 ◯ 11   o) 12 ◯ 10

p) 12 ◯ 6   q) 13 ◯ 5   r) 14 ◯ 7

s) 15 ◯ 5   t) 11 ◯ 2   u) 10 ◯ 2

PA3-4: Counting Backwards *(continued)*

2. Find the gap between the numbers by counting backwards on your fingers.

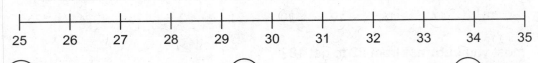

a) 32 ⭕(- 4) 28   b) 31 ⭕ 29   c) 32 ⭕ 27

d) 31 ⭕ 27   e) 30 ⭕ 26   f) 33 ⭕ 26

g) 28 ⭕ 26   h) 32 ⭕ 25   i) 34 ⭕ 26

3. Find the gap between the numbers by counting backwards on your fingers.

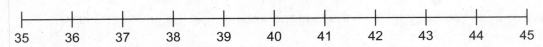

a) 43 ⭕(- 4) 39   b) 41 ⭕ 39   c) 43 ⭕ 37

d) 41 ⭕ 38   e) 40 ⭕ 36   f) 42 ⭕ 35

g) 41 ⭕ 37   h) 45 ⭕ 38   i) 44 ⭕ 36

4. Find the gap between the numbers by counting backwards on your fingers (or by using your subtraction facts).

a) 56 ⭕ 51   b) 59 ⭕ 57   c) 50 ⭕ 48

d) 68 ⭕ 61   e) 60 ⭕ 58   f) 70 ⭕ 68

g) 72 ⭕ 68   h) 81 ⭕ 79   i) 83 ⭕ 78

j) 128 ⭕ 125   k) 167 ⭕ 162   l) 181 ⭕ 178

Patterns & Algebra 1

PA3-4: Counting Backwards (continued)

What number **subtracted** from 8 gives 5?

$8 - \boxed{?} = 5$

Rita puts her finger on 8 on a **number line**.

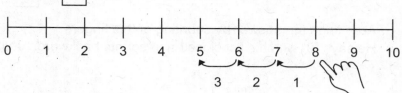

She counts (backward 3 spaces to 5)
to find the number of spaces between 8 and 5.

so: $8 - \boxed{3} = 5$ and: 5 is 3 **less than** 8

----

5. Use the number line to find the <u>difference</u> between the two numbers. Write your answer in the box.

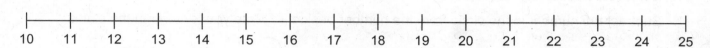

a) $17 - \boxed{} = 14$

b) $15 - \boxed{} = 13$

c) $21 - \boxed{} = 18$

d) $17 - \boxed{} = 12$

e) $19 - \boxed{} = 14$

f) $17 - \boxed{} = 13$

g) $18 - \boxed{} = 16$

h) $21 - \boxed{} = 20$

i) $24 - \boxed{} = 21$

j) $20 - \boxed{} = 14$

k) $21 - \boxed{} = 17$

l) $19 - \boxed{} = 13$

m) $15 - \boxed{} = 12$

n) $16 - \boxed{} = 14$

o) $18 - \boxed{} = 14$

p) $21 - \boxed{} = 15$

q) $20 - \boxed{} = 12$

r) $17 - \boxed{} = 16$

BONUS
6. Fill in the missing number.

a) 17 is _____ less than 20

b) 11 is _____ less than 15

c) 16 is _____ less than 21

d) 19 is _____ less than 21

e) 18 is _____ less than 24

f) 15 is _____ less than 22

g) 14 is _____ less than 19

h) 13 is _____ less than 21

i) 12 is _____ less than 15

Patterns & Algebra 1

PA3-5: Preparation for Decreasing Sequences

What number is 3 **less than** 9? $9 - 3 = \boxed{?}$

Aron finds the answer by counting on his fingers.
He says "9" with his fist closed and counts backwards until he has raised 3 fingers.

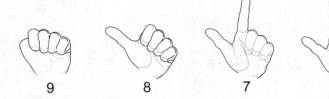

9   8   7   6

The number 6 is 3 **less than** 9.

- -

1. Subtract the number in the circle from the number beside it. Write your answer in the blank.

a) 5 ⊘-2 _____   b) 9 ⊘-3 _____   c) 8 ⊘-4 _____   d) 7 ⊘-1 _____

e) 7 ⊘-5 _____   f) 6 ⊘-4 _____   g) 3 ⊘-1 _____   h) 11 ⊘-2 _____

i) 10 ⊘-6 _____   j) 13 ⊘-2 _____   k) 19 ⊘-4 _____   l) 18 ⊘-3 _____

BONUS

m) 28 ⊘-4 _____   n) 35 ⊘-6 _____   o) 57 ⊘-8 _____   p) 62 ⊘-4 _____

q) 87 ⊘-4 _____   r) 48 ⊘-2 _____   s) 92 ⊘-5 _____   t) 100 ⊘-3 _____

2. Fill in the missing numbers.

a) _____ is 4 less than 7   b) _____ is 2 less than 9   c) _____ is 3 less than 8

d) _____ is 5 less than 17   e) _____ is 4 less than 20   f) _____ is 6 less than 25

g) _____ is 7 less than 28   h) _____ is 4 less than 32   i) _____ is 5 less than 40

j) _____ is 8 less than 59   k) _____ is 6 less than 63   l) _____ is 4 less than 78

1. Extend the **decreasing** patterns.
   NOTE: It is important to start by finding the gap between the numbers.

   Example:

   11 , 9 , 7 , ____ , ____ , ____

   Step 1:

   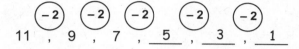

   11 , 9 , 7 , ____ , ____ , ____

   Step 2:

   11 , 9 , 7 , _5_ , _3_ , _1_

a) 10 , 9 , 8 , ____ , ____ , ____

b) 14 , 12 , 10 , ____ , ____ , ____

c) 23 , 22 , 21 , ____ , ____ , ____

d) 24 , 21 , 18 , ____ , ____ , ____

e) 90 , 80 , 70 , ____ , ____ , ____

f) 45 , 40 , 35 , ____ , ____ , ____

g) 15 , 13 , 11 , ____ , ____ , ____

h) 33 , 30 , 27 , ____ , ____ , ____

i) 23 , 21 , 19 , ____ , ____ , ____

j) 28 , 25 , 22 , ____ , ____ , ____

BONUS

k) 95 , 90 , 85 , ____ , ____ , ____

l) 110 , 100 , 90 , ____ , ____ , ____

m) 44 , 40 , 36 , ____ , ____ , ____ , ____ , ____ , ____

PA3-7: Increasing and Decreasing Sequences

1. Extend the patterns, using the gap provided.

Example 1:

(+1)

6 , 7 , _8_ , _9_

Example 2:

(−2)

8 , 6 , _4_ , _2_

(+5)
a) 5 , 10 , ____ , ____

(+3)
b) 2 , 5 , ____ , ____

(+3)
c) 3 , 6 , ____ , ____

(+2)
d) 8 , 10 , ____ , ____

(+2)
e) 14 , 16 , ____ , ____

(+5)
f) 15 , 20 , ____ , ____

(−1)
g) 13 , 12 , ____ , ____

(−2)
h) 18 , 16 , ____ , ____

(−5)
i) 25 , 20 , ____ , ____

(−2)
j) 9 , 7 , ____ , ____

(−3)
k) 22 , 19 , ____ , ____

(−4)
l) 17 , 13 , ____ , ____

(−5)
m) 29 , 24 , ____ , ____

(+5)
n) 32 , 37 , ____ , ____

(+3)
o) 21 , 24 , ____ , ____

(−2)
p) 102 , 100 , ____ , ____

BONUS
2. Rachel has a box of 24 tangerines. She eats 3 each day for 5 days. How many are left?

3. Extend the patterns by first finding the gap.
   HINT: You should first check that the gap is the same between each pair of numbers!

Example:

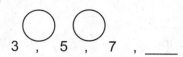

3 , 5 , 7 , ____

Step 1:

(+2) (+2)

3 , 5 , 7 , ____

Step 2:

(+2) (+2)

3 , 5 , 7 , 9

a) 5 , 8 , 11 , ____

b) 2 , 4 , 6 , ____

c) 6 , 10 , 14 , ____

d) 1 , 3 , 5 , ____

e) 21 , 24 , 27 , ____

f) 12 , 17 , 22 , ____

g) 25 , 23 , 21 , ____

h) 29 , 24 , 19 , ____

i) 12 , 9 , 6 , ____ , ____

j) 30 , 25 , 20 , ____ , ____

BONUS

k) 45 , 48 , 51 , ____

l) 105 , 95 , 85 , ____ , ____

m) 32 , 34 , 36 , ____ , ____ , ____ , ____ , ____ , ____ , ____

PA3-8: Attributes

Anne makes a pattern with beads. She uses 4 **shapes**.

cylinder

cone

cube

ball (sphere)

She uses 3 **colours**: red = R
yellow = Y
blue = B

She uses 2 different **sizes**:

big   small

TEACHER:
Make sure students understand that while the cylinders directly above are different sizes, they are still the same shape.

- -

1. Circle the <u>one</u> attribute that changes in each pattern.

    HINT: Check each attribute one at a time. First ask: "Does the <u>shape</u> change?" Then ask: "Does the <u>colour</u> change?" Then ask: "Does the <u>size</u> change?"

a)
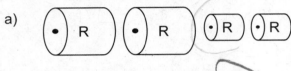
shape   colour   size

b)
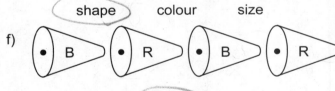
shape   colour   size

c)
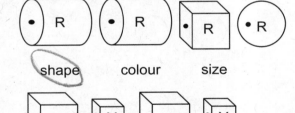
shape   colour   size

d)
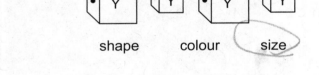
shape   colour   size

e)
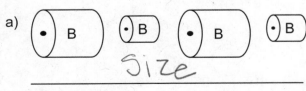
shape   colour   size

f)
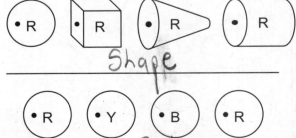
shape   colour   size

2. Write the <u>one</u> attribute that changes in each pattern.

a)
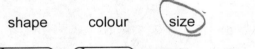
Size

b)
shape

c)
Size

d)

Colour

3. Circle the <u>two</u> attributes that change in each sequence.

a)
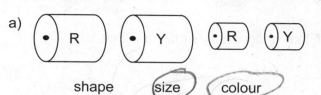

shape   size   colour

b)
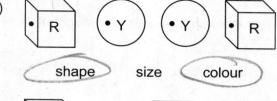

shape   size   colour

c)
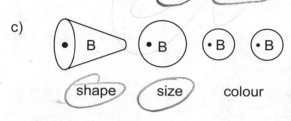

shape   size   colour

d)
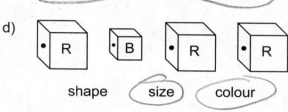

shape   size   colour

4. Write the <u>two</u> attributes that change in each pattern.

a)
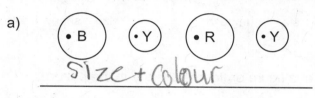

size + colour

b)
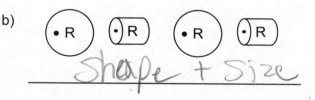

shape + size

c)
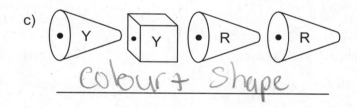

colour + shape

d)
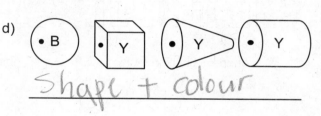

shape + colour

5. Write the <u>one</u>, <u>two</u> or <u>three</u> attributes that change in each sequence.

a)
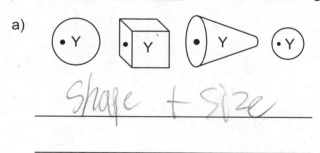

shape + size

b)
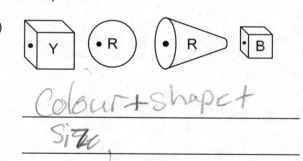

colour + shape + size

c)
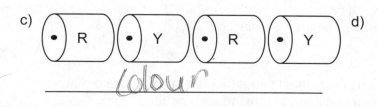

colour

d)
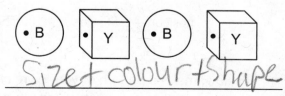

size + colour + shape

PA3-9: Patterns Where Two Attributes Change

To make a pattern, you can change the <u>colour</u>, <u>shape</u>, <u>size</u> or <u>position</u> of a figure, or you can change the <u>number</u> of times a figure occurs.

1. Circle the word that tells you which attribute of a figure or figures changes in the pattern.

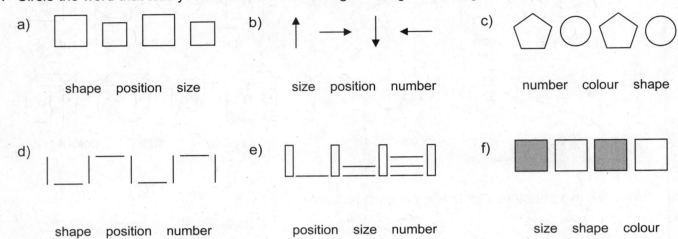

a)

    shape   position   size

b)

    size   position   number

c)

    number   colour   shape

d)

    shape   position   number

e)

    position   size   number

f)

    size   shape   colour

2. Circle the <u>two</u> words that tell you which attributes of a figure or figures change in the pattern.

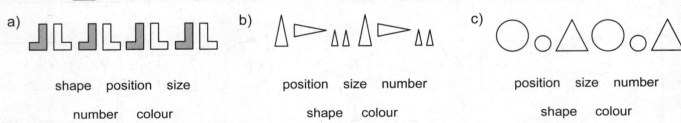

a)

    shape   position   size

    number   colour

b)

    position   size   number

    shape   colour

c)

    position   size   number

    shape   colour

3. Circle the <u>three</u> words that tell you which attributes of a figure or figures change in the pattern.

a)

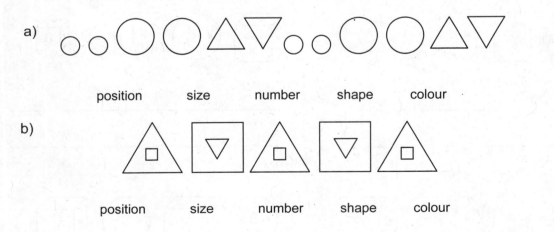

    position   size   number   shape   colour

b)

    position   size   number   shape   colour

4. Below, make a pattern of your own, changing at least two attributes in the figure or figures. In your notebook, explain which attributes you used in making your pattern.

PA3-10: Repeating Patterns

Kevin makes a **repeating** pattern using blocks.

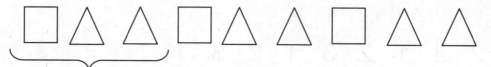

This is the core of Kevin's pattern.

The **core** of a pattern is the part that repeats.

---

1. Circle the <u>core</u> of the following patterns.

a)

b)

c)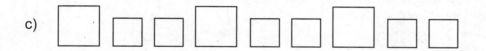

d)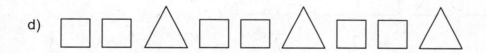

e)

f)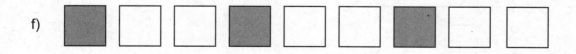

g)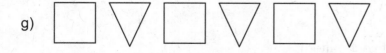

h)

PA3-10: Repeating Patterns *(continued)*

i) A B B A B B A B B

j) 1 2 3 1 2 3 1 2 3 1

k) 1 2 3 4 5 1 2 3 4 5 1 2 3

l) 9 9 7 7 9 9 7 7 9 9 7

m)

n) A B C A B C A B C A B

BONUS

o)

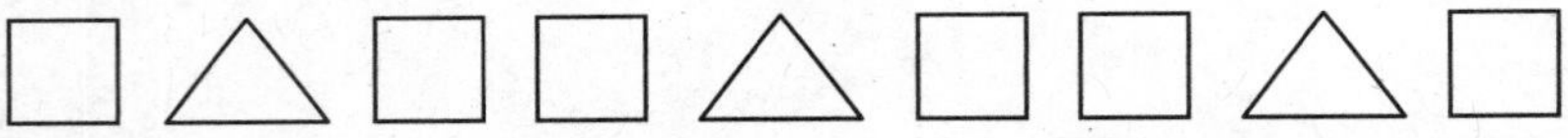

p) A B A A B A A B A A

q)

r) 2 1 2 2 1 2 2 1 2

2. Draw a repeating pattern of your own.
   Ask another student to identify the core of your pattern.

3. Circle the <u>core</u> of the pattern. Then continue the pattern.

a) □ △ ○ □ △ ○ ___ ___ ___ ___ ___ ___

b) ▨ ▥ □ ▨ ▥ □ ___ ___ ___ ___ ___

c) A B C A B C A ___ ___ ___ ___ ___

d) 2 7 9 5 2 7 9 5 ___ ___ ___ ___ ___

e) 2 0 0 1 2 0 0 1 ___ ___ ___ ___ ___

f) 1 5 1 1 5 1 1 5 1 1 5 ___ ___ ___ ___ ___ ___

g) A B B A A B B A ___ ___ ___ ___ ___ ___

h) 1 2 2 2 1 1 2 2 2 1 1 2 2 ___ ___ ___ ___

i) △ △ △ △ △ △ ___ ___ ___ ___ ___

j) ___ ___ ___ ___ ___

k) ↑ → ↓ ← ↑ → ↓ ← ↑ ___ ___ ___

1. The box shows the core of the pattern Karen made with red (R) and yellow (Y) blocks.
   Continue her pattern.

a)

b)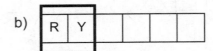

c)

d)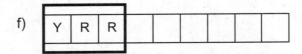

e)

f)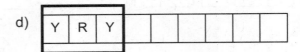

g)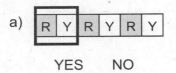

h)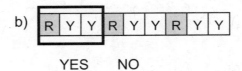

2. The core of Rachel's pattern is in the rectangle.
   Stan tried to continue the pattern.
   Did he continue the pattern correctly?
   HINT: Shade the reds if it helps.

a)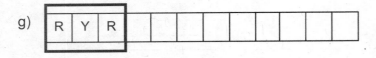

   YES   NO

b)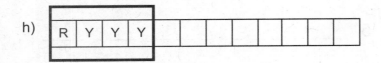

   YES   NO

c)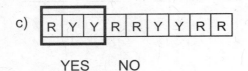

   YES   NO

d)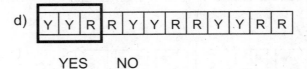

   YES   NO

e)

   YES   NO

f)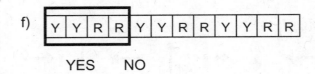

   YES   NO

1. Are the blocks in the rectangle the <u>core</u> of the pattern?

a) `[R Y] R Y R Y`

   YES   NO

b) `[R Y Y] R Y Y R Y Y`

   YES   NO

c) `[R Y Y] R R Y Y R`

   YES   NO

d) `[Y Y R] R Y Y R R Y Y R R`

   YES   NO

e) `[Y R Y R R] Y R Y R R`

   YES   NO

f) `[R Y] R Y Y R Y R Y Y`

   YES   NO

2. Put a rectangle around the blocks that make up the core.

a) `Y R R Y R R Y R R`

b) `R R R Y R R R Y`

c) `Y Y R R Y Y R R Y Y R R`

d) `Y R R Y Y R R Y`

e) `R Y R Y Y Y R Y R Y Y Y`

f) `R Y R Y R Y R Y R`

g) `Y R Y Y R Y R Y Y R Y R`

h) `R Y Y Y R R Y Y Y R`

3. Continue the pattern below to show 20 blocks altogether.

1	2	3	4	5	6	7	8	9	10	11	12	13	14	15	16	17	18	19	20
R	Y	R	Y	R	Y	R	Y	R	Y										

a) What colour are the following blocks?

   i) block 12   ii) block 14   iii) block 15   iv) block 18

b) What colour are the blocks of the even numbers (2, 4, 6, 8, ...)? _____

c) If you continued the pattern, what colour would the following blocks be?

   i) block 22   ii) block 27   iii) block 35   iv) block 44

1. Add a square to the figure (along the edge shown by the arrow).

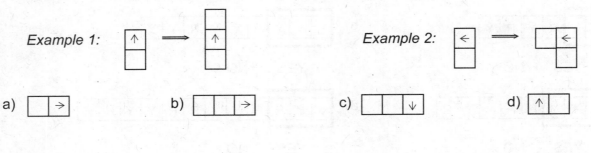

2. Shade the square that was added to Figure 1 to make Figure 2.

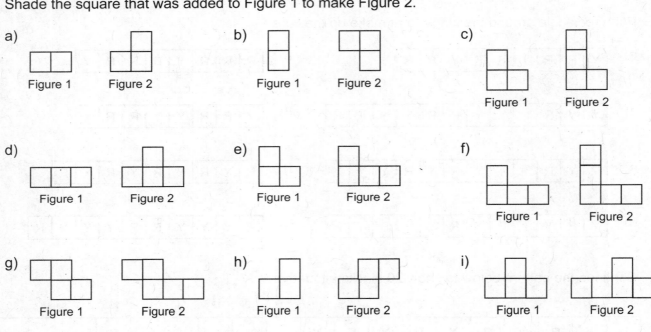

3. Shade the <u>two</u> squares that were added to Figure 1 to make Figure 2.

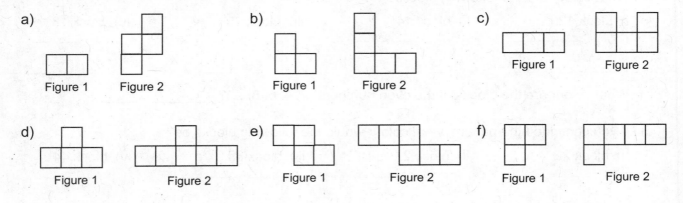

PA3-13: Making Patterns with Squares *(continued)*

4. Shade any squares that were added to make the <u>next</u> figure in the pattern.

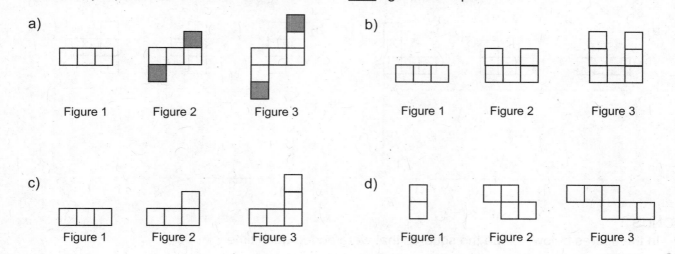

a)

Figure 1   Figure 2   Figure 3

b)

Figure 1   Figure 2   Figure 3

c)

Figure 1   Figure 2   Figure 3

d)

Figure 1   Figure 2   Figure 3

5. Shade any squares that were added to make the next figure.
   Then draw Figure 4 in the box provided.

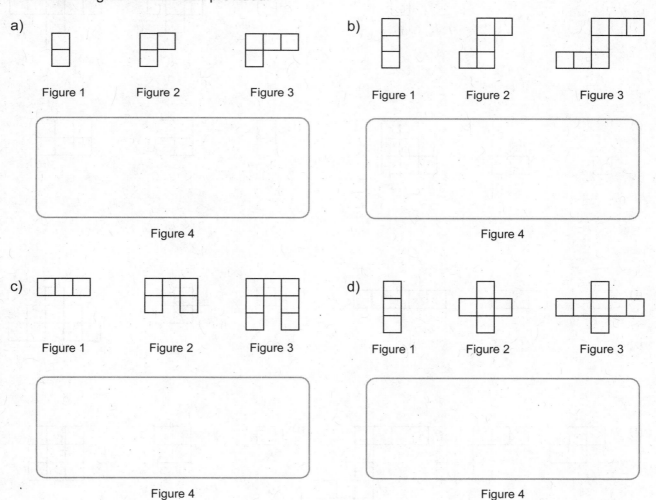

a)

Figure 1   Figure 2   Figure 3

Figure 4

b)

Figure 1   Figure 2   Figure 3

Figure 4

c)

Figure 1   Figure 2   Figure 3

Figure 4

d)

Figure 1   Figure 2   Figure 3

Figure 4

Patterns & Algebra 1

PA3-14: Making Patterns with Squares (Advanced)

1. Draw the next figure (or build it using blocks).

a)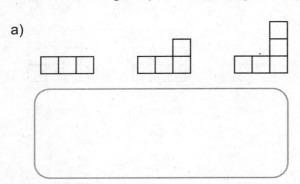

b)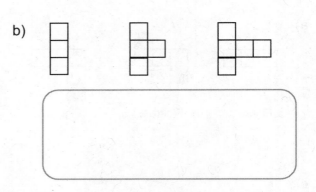

BONUS

2. In the figures below, shade the squares that were added each time.

For an extra challenge draw the next figure on grid paper (or build it with blocks).

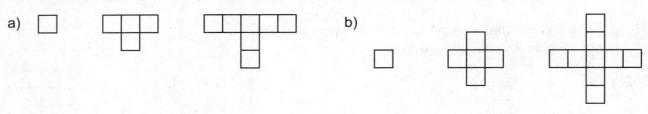

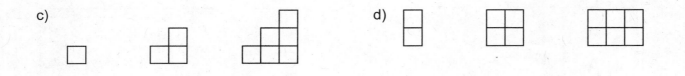

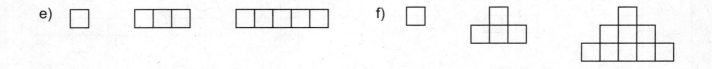

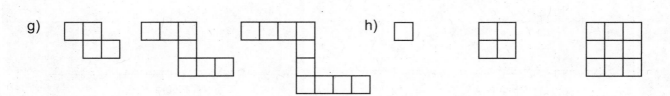

1. Continue the following sequences by <u>adding</u> the number given.

   a) (add 3) 30, 33, _____ , _____ , _____

   b) (add 5) 60, 65, _____ , _____ , _____

   c) (add 2) 26, 28, _____ , _____ , _____

   d) (add 10) 20, 30, _____ , _____ , _____

   e) (add 3) 12, 15, _____ , _____ , _____

   f) (add 5) 46, 51, _____ , _____ , _____

   g) (add 5) 105, 110, _____ , _____ , _____

   h) (add 5) 4, 9, _____ , _____ , _____

2. Continue the following sequences, <u>subtracting</u> by the number given.

   a) (subtract 2) 12, 10, _____ , _____ , _____

   b) (subtract 3) 18, 15, _____ , _____ , _____

   c) (subtract 5) 55, 50, _____ , _____ , _____

   d) (subtract 3) 63, 60, _____ , _____ , _____

   e) (subtract 2) 88, 86, _____ , _____ , _____

   f) (subtract 5) 79, 74, _____ , _____ , _____

   g) (subtract 3) 30, 27, _____ , _____ , _____

   h) (subtract 5) 200, 195, _____ , _____ , _____

BONUS

3. Which of the following sequences were made by adding 3? Circle them.
   HINT: Check all the numbers in the sequence.

   a) 3, 7, 9, 11

   b) 3, 6, 9, 11

   c) 3, 6, 9, 12

   d) 19, 22, 25, 28

   e) 15, 18, 21, 24

   f) 18, 21, 24, 29

4.   **2, 6, 10, 14 ...**

Ann says the above pattern was made by adding 4 each time. Is she right? Explain how you know.

_____

_____

5. Continue the following sequences by <u>adding</u> the number given.

a) (add 4)   30, 34, _____ , _____ , _____

b) (add 9)   11, 20, _____ , _____ , _____

c) (add 6)   10, 16, _____ , _____ , _____

d) (add 7)   70, 77, _____ , _____ , _____

e) (add 11) 10, 21, _____ , _____ , _____

f) (add 4)   56, 60, _____ , _____ , _____

g) (add 8)   73, 81, _____ , _____ , _____

h) (add 10) 71, 81, _____ , _____ , _____

6. Continue the following sequences by <u>subtracting</u> the number given.

a) (subtract 4)   45, 41, _____ , _____ , _____

b) (subtract 7)   48, 41, _____ , _____ , _____

c) (subtract 3)   92, 89, _____ , _____ , _____

d) (subtract 8)   142, 134, _____ , _____ , _____

e) (subtract 5)   230, 225, _____ , _____

f) (subtract 5)   565, 560, _____ , _____

g) (subtract 6)   366, 360, _____ , _____

h) (subtract 10) 423, 413, _____ , _____

BONUS

7. Create a pattern of your own. Write your pattern in the blanks. Then give the rule you used.

_____ , _____ , _____ , _____ , _____   My rule: _____

8.   **67, 59, 51, 43, 35 ...**

Tariq says this sequence was made by subtracting 9 each time. Sharon says it was made by subtracting 8. Who is right?

_____

_____

PA3-16: Identifying Pattern Rules

1. The following sequences were made by <u>adding</u> a number repeatedly. In each case, say what number was added.

   a) 2, 4, 6, 8   add _____   b) 3, 6, 9, 12   add _____

   c) 15, 18, 21, 24   add _____   d) 42, 44, 46, 48   add _____

   e) 41, 46, 51, 56   add _____   f) 19, 23, 27, 31   add _____

   g) 243, 245, 247, 249   add _____   h) 21, 27, 33, 39   add _____

2. The following sequences were made by <u>subtracting</u> a number repeatedly. In each case, say what number was subtracted.

   a) 16, 14, 12, 10   subtract _____   b) 30, 25, 20, 15   subtract _____

   c) 100, 99, 98, 97   subtract _____   d) 42, 39, 36, 33   subtract _____

   e) 17, 14, 11, 8   subtract _____   f) 99, 97, 95, 93   subtract _____

   g) 190, 180, 170, 160   subtract _____   h) 100, 95, 90, 85   subtract _____

3. State the rule for the following patterns.

   a) 117, 110, 103, 96, 89   subtract _____   b) 1, 9, 17, 25, 33, 41   add _____

   c) 101, 105, 109, 113   _____   d) 99, 88, 77, 66   _____

BONUS

4. Continue the pattern by filling in the blanks. Then write a rule for the pattern.

   13, 18, 23, _____, _____, _____   The rule is: _____

5.   **5, 8, 11, 14, 17 ...**

   Keith says the pattern rule is: "Start at 5 and subtract 3 each time."

   Jane says the rule is: "Add 4 each time."

   Molly says the rule is: "Start at 5 and add 3 each time."

   a) Whose rule is correct?

   b) What mistakes did the others make? Explain.

PA3-17: Introduction to T-tables

Abdul makes a **growing** pattern with squares. He records the number of squares in each figure in a T-table. He also records the number of squares he adds each time he makes a new figure.

  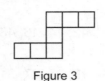

Figure 1   Figure 2   Figure 3

Figure	# of Squares	
1	3	
2	5	② ← Number of squares
3	7	② ← added each time

The number of squares in the figures are 3, 5, 7, …
Abdul writes a rule for this number pattern.
RULE: Start at 3 and add 2 each time.

----

1. Abdul makes another <u>growing</u> pattern with squares. How many squares does he add to make each new figure? Write your answer in the circles provided. Then write a rule for the pattern.

a)

Figure	Number of Squares
1	4
2	7
3	10

Rule:

b)

Figure	Number of Squares
1	2
2	5
3	8

Rule:

c)

Figure	Number of Squares
1	4
2	6
3	8

Rule:

d)

Figure	Number of Squares
1	1
2	5
3	9

Rule:

e)

Figure	Number of Squares
1	5
2	7
3	9

Rule:

f)

Figure	Number of Squares
1	6
2	12
3	18

Rule:

g)

Figure	Number of Squares
1	2
2	8
3	14

Rule:

h)

Figure	Number of Squares
1	3
2	6
3	9

Rule:

i)

Figure	Number of Squares
1	5
2	12
3	19

Rule:

BONUS

2. Extend the number pattern. How many squares would be used in Figure 6?

a)

Figure	Number of Squares
1	2
2	5
3	8
4	
5	
6	

b)

Figure	Number of Squares
1	6
2	9
3	12

c)

Figure	Number of Squares
1	1
2	6
3	11

d)

Figure	Number of Squares
1	4
2	9
3	14

e)

Figure	Number of Squares
1	10
2	13
3	16

f)

Figure	Number of Squares
1	12
2	16
3	20

3. Make a T-table and record the number of squares or circles in each figure. Write a rule for the pattern.

a)

b)

4. Amy makes a growing pattern with squares. After making Figure 3, she only has 14 squares left. Does she have enough squares to complete Figure 4?

a)

Figure	Number of Squares
1	4
2	7
3	10

YES   NO

b)

Figure	Number of Squares
1	6
2	9
3	12

YES   NO

c)

Figure	Number of Squares
1	1
2	6
3	11

YES   NO

5. Extend the pattern to find out how many eggs 5 birds would lay.

a)

Bald Eagle	Number of Eggs
1	2
2	4
3	
4	
5	

b)

Sand-piper	Number of Eggs
1	4
2	8

c)

Snow Goose	Number of Eggs
1	3
2	6

d)

Marsh Hawk	Number of Eggs
1	5
2	10

6. How many young would 5 animals have?

a)

Polar Bear	Number of Cubs
1	2
2	4

b)

Swift Fox	Number of Pups
1	4
2	8

c)

Bearded Seal	Number of Pups
1	5
2	10

d)

Coyote	Number of Cubs
1	6
2	12

7. How much money would Alice earn for 4 hours of work?

a)

Hours Worked	Dollars Earned in an Hour
1	$7

b)

Hours Worked	Dollars Earned in an Hour
1	$8

c)

Hours Worked	Dollars Earned in an Hour
1	$6

Answer the following questions in your notebook.

1. How many squares or triangles would be used for Figure 6? Explain how you know.

   a)

   b)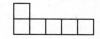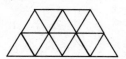

   c)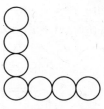

   d)

2. Priya makes a sequence of Ls with nickels.

   Figure 1   Figure 2   Figure 3

   a) How many nickels will be in Figure 5?

   b) What is the value of the coins in Figure 5?

3. Indra makes broaches with triangles. She has 16 triangles.

   Does she have enough triangles to make 5 broaches if there are …

   a)

   4 triangles in
   each broach?

   b)

   3 triangles in
   each broach?

   c)

   6 triangles in
   each broach?

   d) Explain how you know the answer for part a).

BONUS

4. The even numbers (greater than 0) are the numbers you say when counting by 2s:

   2, 4, 6, 8, 10, 12, 14 ...

   Predict whether the number of squares in Figure 10 in Question 1 d) above will be even or not.

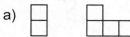

PA3-19: Problems and Puzzles

Answer the following questions in your notebook.

1. Bill saves $6 each month.

   a) How much he will save in 3 months?

   b) How many months will it take him to save $30?

2. It costs $5 to rent a kayak for the first hour.
   It costs $4 for each hour after that.

   a) How much does it cost to rent the kayak for 4 hours?

   b) Sandra has $26. Can she rent the kayak for 6 hours?

3. Karla has 20 toothpicks.
   Can she make a design with 6 squares?
   Explain how you know.

 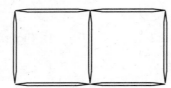 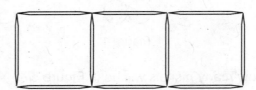

Step 1	**Step 2**	**Step 3**

4. How many squares and circles would be in Design E?

 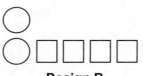 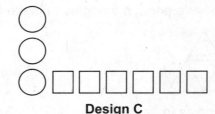

Design A	**Design B**	**Design C**

5. Each pattern was made by adding a number repeatedly.
   Find the mistake and correct it.

   a) 5, 8, 9, 11, 13

   b) 7, 10, 13, 15, 19

6. Find an increasing pattern and a repeating pattern in your classroom.

jump math
MULTIPLYING POTENTIAL.

Patterns & Algebra 1

1. Write the place value of the underlined digit.

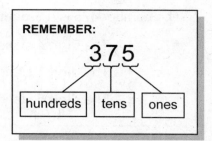

REMEMBER:

375

hundreds | tens | ones

a) 1<u>7</u>   ones

b) 9<u>8</u>

c) <u>2</u>4

d) 6<u>3</u>

e) <u>3</u>81

f) 97<u>2</u>

g) 4<u>5</u>7

h) 7<u>9</u>

i) <u>2</u>61

j) <u>8</u>

2. Give the place value of the number 5 in each of the numbers below.
   HINT: Underline the 5 in each question first.

a) 50

b) 15

c) 251

d) 586

e) 375

f) 584

3. You can also write numbers using a place value chart.

Example:

In a place value chart, 431 is:

hundreds	tens	ones
4	3	1

Write the following numbers into the place value chart.

	hundreds	tens	ones
a) 65	0	6	5
b) 283			
c) 17			
d) 942			
e) 408			

	hundreds	tens	ones
f) 130			
g) 753			
h) 4			
i) 201			
j) 989			

jump math
MULTIPLYING POTENTIAL.

Number Sense 1

The number 475 is a **3-digit number**.

- The **digit** 4 stands for 400 – the **value** of the digit 4 is 400.
- The **digit** 7 stands for 70 – the **value** of the digit 7 is 70.
- The **digit** 5 stands for 5 – the **value** of the digit 5 is 5.

---

1. Write the **value** of each digit.

a)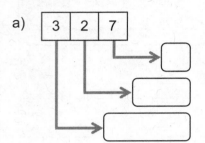

b)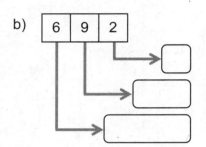

c)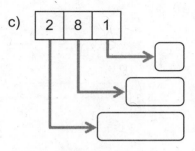

2. What does the digit 3 stand for in each number? The first one is done for you.

a)   237

   30

b)   523

c)   638

d)   326

e)   403

f)   732

g)   309

h)   883

i)   321

j)   203

k)   532

l)   937

3. Fill in the blanks.

a) In the number 657, the **digit** 5 stands for _____ .

b) In the number 248, the **digit** 2 stands for _____ .

c) In the number 129 the **digit** 1 stand for _____ .

d) In the number 380, the **value** of the digit 8 is _____ .

e) In the number 267, the **value** of the digit 7 is _____ .

f) In the number 847 the **value** of the digit 8 is _____ .

g) In the number 803, the digit _____ is in the **hundreds place**.

h) In the number 596, the digit _____ is in the **tens place**.

i) In the number 401, the digit _____ is in the **tens place**.

1. Circle the pair of numbers that starts with same sound.

   a)   (two)   fifteen   (twelve)   b)   thirteen   three   fifteen

         2   15   12   13   3   15

2. Write numbers for the number words.

   a) (nineteen) = __ __   b) (eighteen) = __ __

   c) (sixteen) = __ __   d) (fifteen) = __ __

   e) (thirteen) = __ __   f) (twelve) = __ __

   g) (seventy) = __ __   h) (fifty) = __ __

   i) (eighty) = __ __   j) (forty) = __ __

3. Write the word ending for each numeral.

   a) 60 = six ty_____   b) 16 = six_____   c) 40 = for_____

   d) 14 = four_____   e) 50 = fif_____   f) 20 = twen_____

   g) 13 = thir_____   h) 18 = eight_____   i) 70 = seven_____

4. Cover up your work in Questions 2 and 3. Write words for the numerals.

   a) 70 = _____   b) 60 = _____   c) 90 = _____

   d) 17 = ___seventeen___   e) 16 = _____   f) 19 = _____

   g) 40 = _____   h) 50 = _____   i) 30 = _____

   j) 14 = _____   k) 15 = _____   l) 13 = _____

jump math
MULTIPLYING POTENTIAL.

Number Sense 1

1. Write numerals for the following words.

   a) six _____   b) eight _____   c) nine _____

   d) thirty-two _____   e) seventy-five _____   f) eighty-two _____

   g) two hundred six _____   h) three hundred twelve _____

   i) four hundred sixty-seven _____

   j) six hundred forty-nine _____

Number Words for the Ones Place	
zero	five
one	six
two	seven
three	eight
four	nine

2. Write the number words for the numerals.

   a) 2 _____   b) 5 _____

   c) 17 _____   d) 12 _____

   e) 22 _____   f) 73 _____

   g) 37 _____   h) 64 _____

Number Words for the Teens	
eleven	sixteen
twelve	seventeen
thirteen	eighteen
fourteen	nineteen
fifteen	

3. Writing numbers 100 to 999.

   Step 1:   Underline the left-most digit.   Write its value.

   a) <u>4</u> 3 5   four hundred _____

   b) 2 3 7   _____

   c) 5 2 1   _____

Number Words for the Tens Place	
ten	sixty
twenty	seventy
thirty	eighty
forty	ninety
fifty	

   Step 2:   Cover the left-most digit.   Write the number words for the remaining digits.

   d) 6 8 2   six hundred   eighty-two _____

   e) 7 9 3   seven hundred _____

   f) 8 5 1   eight hundred _____

4. Write number words for the following numerals.

   a) 121 _____

   b) 307 _____

   c) 698 _____

   d) 846 _____

   e) 913 _____

5. Underline the number word or words in each sentence.

   a) Paula has three pet fish.

   b) Keiko bought thirty grapes.

   c) A bus can hold sixty-four children.

   d) Pat ran three kilometres in forty-five minutes.

   e) Jerome will be nine years old in two weeks.

6. In each blank write a number word that would make sense.

   a) There are _____ days in a week and _____ hours in a day.

   b) There are _____ boys and _____ girls in a grade _____ class.

   c) In the last _____ hours, I ate _____ meals.

   d) I can run non-stop for _____ minutes.

   e) I can hold my breath for _____ seconds.

7. Write the numbers provided in words on the signs where they are missing.

   a)

   FOR SALE

   (8) _____ kittens.

   b)
   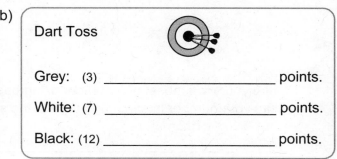

   Dart Toss

   Grey: (3) _____ points.

   White: (7) _____ points.

   Black: (12) _____ points.

1. What number is shown in the picture?

   Write your answer in **expanded form** (as shown in the example).

   Example:

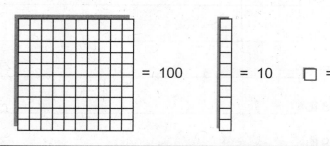

Base ten blocks are used to represent ones, tens, and hundreds:

= 100   = 10   □ = 1

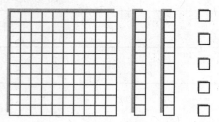

__1__ hundreds + __2__ tens + __5__ ones =   125

a)

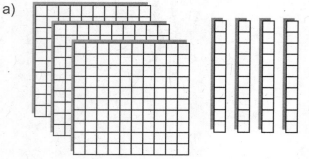

___ hundreds + ___ tens + ___ ones =

b)

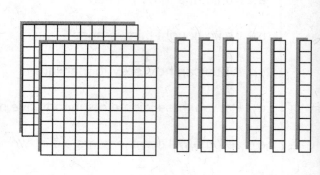

___ hundreds + ___ tens + ___ ones =

c)

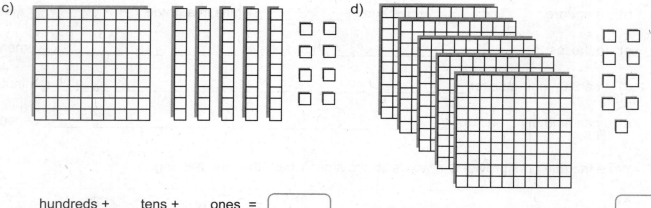

___ hundreds + ___ tens + ___ ones =

d)

___ hundreds + ___ tens + ___ ones =

BONUS

2. Make your own model of a number using base ten blocks.
   Write your number in expanded form in the space below.

3. Using the chart paper below, draw base ten models for the following numbers.
   (Be sure to make your models the right size!)

   The first one has been done for you.

a) 147

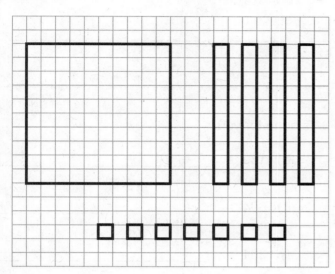

b) 63

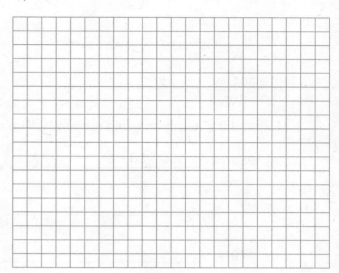

c) 405

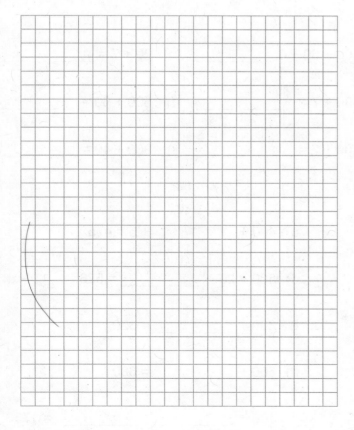

d) 98

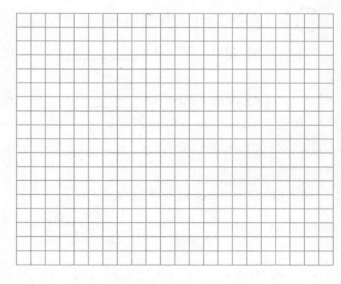

 4. Draw base ten models for …

      a) 327   b) 200   c) 52

1. Expand the following numbers in numerals and words.

    a) 427 = __4__ hundreds + __2__ tens + __7__ ones   b) 893 = ____ hundreds + ____ tens + ____ ones

    c) 56 = ____ hundreds + ____ tens + ____ ones   d) 2   = ____ hundreds + ____ tens + ____ ones

    e) 671 = _____

    f) 304 = _____

2. Expand the numbers using numerals. The first one is done for you.

    a) 953 = __900 + 50 + 3_____   b) 139 = _____

    c) 27 = _____   d) 604 = _____

    e) 470 = _____   f) 201 = _____

    g) 32 = _____   h) 493 = _____

3. Write the number for each sum.

    a) 200 + 50 + 3 = _____   b) 400 + 60 + 8 = _____   c) 20 + 7 = _____

    d) 900 + 90 + 9 = _____   e) 600 + 7 = _____   f) 500 + 60 = _____

    g) 300 + 20 + 7 = _____   h) 800 + 2 = _____   i) 900 + 40 = _____

4. Find the missing numbers.

    a) 800 + _____ + 7 = 827   b) 400 + _____ + 5 = 475

    c) 900 + _____ + 2 = 982   d) 500 + 20 + _____ = 526

    e) 200 + _____ = 202   f) 300 + _____ = 320

    g) _____ + 30 = 730   h) 600 + _____ = 680

    i) 900 + _____ + _____ = 926   j) 100 + _____ + _____ = 173

5. Write each number in **expanded form**. Then draw a base ten model.

Example: 634 =   600 + 30 + 4

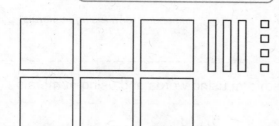

HINT:
Don't worry about drawing the models in too much detail.
Use a large square for hundreds, a strip for tens and a small square for ones.

a) 317 =

b) 65 =

c) 446 =

d) 202 =

e) 130 =

f) 24 =

6. George has ...

- 100 stamps from Canada,
- 50 stamps from England, and
- 6 stamps from Portugal.

How many stamps does he have in total? Explain how you know.

Patrick makes a **model** of the number 27 using base ten blocks.
He writes the number in **expanded form**, using **words and numerals**, and using **numerals alone**.

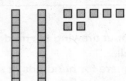

27 = 2 tens + 7 ones   *expanded form (using words and numerals)*

27 = 20 + 7   *expanded form (using numerals)*

---

1. Draw a model. Write the number in expanded form using words _and_ using numerals.

a) 32
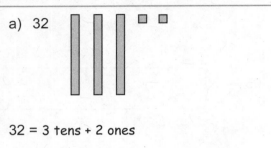

32 = 3 tens + 2 ones

32 = 30 + 2

b) 43

43 =

43 =

c) 52

52 =

52 =

d) 16

16 =

16 =

2. Write numerals for the following number words.

a) twenty-six _____   b) seventeen _____   c) thirty-two _____   d) sixty-seven _____

e) thirty-six _____   f) eighty-five _____   g) seventy-six _____   h) forty-four _____

i) ninety-two _____   j) forty _____   k) seventy-nine _____   l) fifty-one _____

3. Write number words for the following numerals.

a) 26   twenty-six   b) 32   c) 376   d) 21   e) 269   f) 54

BONUS

4. Represent the number 53 with a model, with number words, and in expanded form (2 ways).

Compare the base ten models to determine which amount is greater.

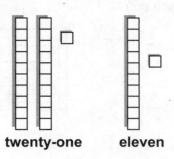 = 10   □ = 1   *Example:*

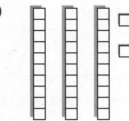 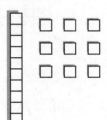

twenty-one   **eleven**

> **HINT:** Count the number of tens first! The number with <u>more tens</u> is greater.

twenty-one: **2** tens
eleven: **1** ten

So, twenty-one is greater than eleven.

---

1. Circle the greater number in each pair. The first one has been done for you.

a)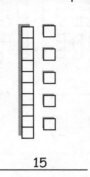

_____ 23 _____   _____ 15 _____

b)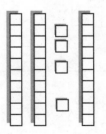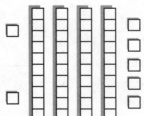

_____   _____

> **NOTE:** The first number is greater because it has <u>2</u> tens blocks and the other only has <u>1</u>.

2. Circle the greater number in each pair. Write the **names** of each number in words. Be sure to check your spelling! Then circle the greater number.

a)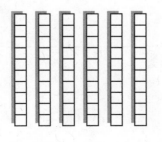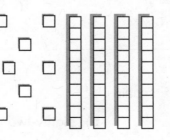

_____   _____

b)

_____   _____

> **TEACHER:**
> **Make the words below a regular part of your spelling lessons:**
>
> | | |
> |---|---|
> | one | |
> | two | twenty |
> | three | thirty |
> | four | forty |
> | five | fifty |
> | six | sixty |
> | seven | seventy |
> | eight | eighty |
> | nine | ninety |
> | ten | one hundred |

3. Write a number for each model in the box. Write the words for each number on the line below. Then, circle the greater number in each pair.

a)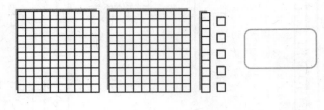

_____   _____

b)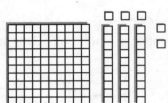

_____   _____

4. Explain how you knew which number in Question 3 a) was greater.

_____

_____

5. Write words for each number. Then circle the greater number in each pair.
   HINT: If there is the same number of hundreds, count the number of tens.

a)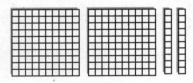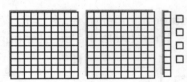

_____   _____

b)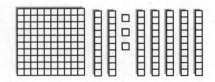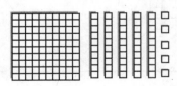

_____   _____

6. Circle the greater number in each pair.

a) 34   forty-two   b) eighty-two   91   c) fifty-six   63

d) three hundred six   217   e) one hundred thirty-two   140

1. Write the **value** of each digit. Then complete the sentence.

    a) 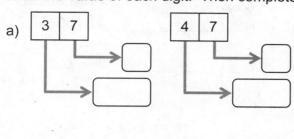   b)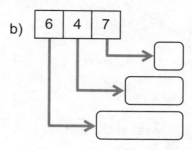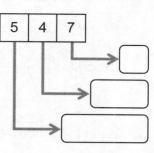

    _____ is greater than _____   _____ is greater than _____

2. Circle the pair of digits that are different in each pair of numbers.
    Then write the greater number in the box.

    a) 4 7 5   b) 3 6 0   c) 8 5 2   d) 1 3 6
        4 6 5   2 6 0   8 5 8   1 2 6

    [475]   [   ]   [   ]   [   ]

3. Read the numbers from left to right.
    Circle the first pair of digits you find that are different. Then write the greater number in the box.

    a) 5 8 3   b) 6 2 9   c) 5 7 6   d) 4 3 2
        5 9 7   6 5 4   6 0 3   4 3 1

    [597]   [   ]   [   ]   [   ]

    e) 3 8 4   f) 9 0 6   g) 8 7 5   h) 2 3 8
        5 9 7   9 0 4   8 6 9   2 2 1

    [   ]   [   ]   [   ]   [   ]

4. Circle the greater number.
    a) 111 or 311   b) 625 or 525   c) 321 or 721

    d) 843 or 867   e) 480 or 412   f) 219 or 220

    g) 125 or 122   h) 854 or 859   i) 336 or 330

5. a) Sindi earns $18 an hour. Bianca earns $13 an hour. Who earns more?

    _____

    b) Anthony's grandfather is 83. Nita's grandfather is 81. Whose grandfather is older?

    _____

 jump math
MULTIPLYING POTENTIAL

Number Sense 1

1. Write "10 more" or "10 less" in the blanks.

   a) 80 is _____ than 70

   b) 20 is _____ than 30

   c) 50 is _____ than 60

   d) 90 is _____ than 80

2. Write "100 more" or "100 less" in the blanks.

   a) 500 is _____ than 400

   b) 300 is _____ than 400

   c) 700 is _____ than 600

   d) 800 is _____ than 900

3. Write the value of the digits. Then say how much more or less the first number is than the second.

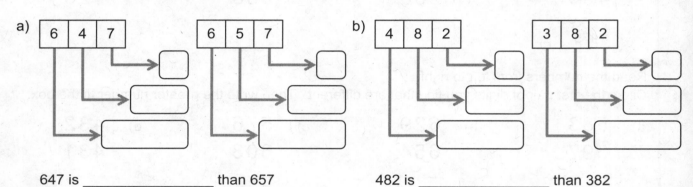

   a) | 6 | 4 | 7 | | 6 | 5 | 7 |

   b) | 4 | 8 | 2 | | 3 | 8 | 2 |

   647 is _____ than 657

   482 is _____ than 382

4. Circle the pair of digits that are different. Then fill in the blanks.

   a) 265
       275

       265 is ____10 less____

       than 275

   b) 392
       492

       392 is _____

       than 492

   c) 687
       677

       687 is _____

       than 677

   d) 362
       262

       362 is _____

       than 262

   e) 405
       415

       405 is _____

       than 415

   f) 587
       687

       587 is _____

       than 687

5. Fill in the blanks.

a) _____ is 10 more than 475

b) _____ is 10 less than 263

c) _____ is 10 less than 387

d) _____ is 10 more than 482

e) _____ is 100 more than 563

f) _____ is 100 less than 402

g) _____ is 100 more than 687

h) _____ is 100 less than 291

i) _____ is 100 less than 305

j) _____ is 100 more than 851

6. Fill in the blanks.

a) 375 + 10 = _____

b) 252 + 10 = _____

c) 972 + 10 = _____

d) 127 + 100 = _____

e) 863 + 100 = _____

f) 821 + 100 = _____

g) 357 – 10 = _____

h) 683 – 10 = _____

i) 932 – 10 = _____

j) 487 – 100 = _____

k) 901 – 100 = _____

l) 316 – 100 = _____

m) 301 – 10 = _____

n) 507 – 10 = _____

o) 397 – 10 = _____

7. Fill in the blanks.

a) 385 + _____ = 395

b) 201 + _____ = 301

c) 483 + _____ = 493

d) 617 + _____ = 717

e) 286 – _____ = 276

f) 837 – _____ = 737

BONUS

8. Continue the number patterns.

a) 508, 518, 528, _____, _____

b) 572, 672, 772, _____, _____

c) 482, 492, _____, 512, _____

d) 363, _____, _____, 393, 403

9. Circle the pair of digits that are different. Then fill in the blanks.

a) 2④1
    2③1

b) 485
    585

c) 682
    692

___231___ is ___10___

_____ is _____

_____ is _____

less than ___241___

greater than _____

less than _____

NS3-11: Comparing Numbers (Advanced)

1. Circle the greater number in each pair.

   a) 35   or   thirty-two   b) eighty-eight   or   91   c) seventy-six   or   71

   d) 99   or   ninety   e) 42   or   fifty-five   f) eleven   or   21

   g) one hundred six   or   107   h) 375   or   three hundred eighty-five

2. List the two-digit numbers you can make using one or both digits.

   a) 4 and 5   b) 6 and 1   c) 3 and 9   d) 6 and 7

3. Create the largest possible **two-digit** number using the digits given.

   a) 3, 2 [ ]   b) 8, 9 [ ]   c) 4, 1 [ ]   d) 7, 4 [ ]

4. Use the digits to create the greatest number and the least number.

   a)

Digits	Greatest Number	Least Number
5 7 2		

   b)

Digits	Greatest Number	Least Number
3 6 2		

5. Arrange the numbers in order, starting with the **least** number.

   a) 75, 62, 87   b) 251, 385, 256

   _____ , _____ , _____   _____ , _____ , _____

   c) 395, 385, 327, 357   d) 432, 484, 402, 434

   _____ , _____ , _____ , _____   _____ , _____ , _____ , _____

6. Arrange the lengths of these ocean animals from shortest to longest.

 13 m    4 m   14 m   30 m

   Giant Squid   Tiger Shark   Whale Shark   Giant Blue Whale

7. List all the **three-digit** numbers you can make using the digits 5, 3 and 2.
   (Use each digit only once in a number.)
   What is the largest number you can make?
   Explain how you know.

1. a) Underline the ones digits of the numbers you say when counting by 2s.

1	2	3	4	5	6	7	8	9	10
11	12	13	14	15	16	17	18	19	20
21	22	23	24	25	26	27	28	29	30
31	32	33	34	35	36	37	38	39	40

The **even** numbers are the numbers you say when counting by 2s (i.e. 0, 2, 4, 6, 8, …).

b) What pattern do you see in the ones digits of the even numbers?

_____

c) Using the pattern continue the following sequences.

   i) 46, 48, 50, _____, _____, _____   ii) 76, 78, 80, _____, _____, _____

   iii) 52, 54, 56, _____, _____, _____   iv) 80, 82, 84, _____, _____, _____

2. a) Underline the ones digits of the numbers you don't say when counting by 2s.

1	2	3	4	5	6	7	8	9	10
11	12	13	14	15	16	17	18	19	20
21	22	23	24	25	26	27	28	29	30
31	32	33	34	35	36	37	38	39	40

The **odd** numbers are the numbers you don't say when counting by 2s (i.e. 1, 3, 5, 7, …).

b) What pattern do you see in the ones digits of the odd numbers?

_____

c) Using the pattern continue the following sequences.

   i) 47, 49, 51, _____, _____, _____   ii) 67, 69, 71, _____, _____, _____

   iii) 53, 55, 57, _____, _____, _____   iv) 81, 83, 85, _____, _____, _____

1. Start at 23. Mark the numbers you say when counting on by 5s. Underline the ones digit.

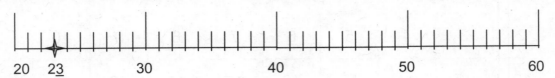

20　23　　　30　　　　40　　　　50　　　　60

What pattern do you see in the underlined ones digits?

_____

2. Here are some number sequences formed by counting by 5s. Underline the ones digit in each number, then write the pattern.

a) 1<u>2</u>, 1<u>7</u>, 2<u>2</u>, 2<u>7</u>, 3<u>2</u>, 3<u>7</u>　　　Pattern in the ones digits: _2_ , ___ , ___ , ___ , ___ , ___

b) 7<u>1</u>, 76, 81, 86, 91, 96　　　Pattern in the ones digits: _1_ , ___ , ___ , ___ , ___ , ___

c) 8<u>4</u>, 89, 94, 99, 104, 109　　　Pattern in the ones digits: _4_ , ___ , ___ , ___ , ___ , ___

3. Complete the number sequence below by counting on by 5s.

a) 29, 34, _____, _____, _____

b) 79, 84, _____, _____, _____

c) 43, 48, _____, _____, _____

d) 56, 61, _____, _____, _____

e) 31, 36, _____, _____, _____

f) 82, 87, _____, _____, _____

g) 107, 112, _____, _____, _____

h) 213, 218, _____, _____, _____

4. Explain what all the patterns above have in common.

5. Start at 25. Circle the numbers you say when counting by 25s.

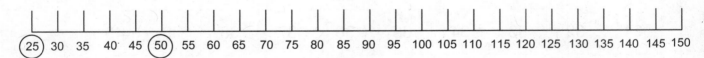

㉕ 30 35 40 45 ㊿ 55 60 65 70 75 80 85 90 95 100 105 110 115 120 125 130 135 140 145 150

Write the pattern in the <u>ones</u> digits of the numbers you circled:

_5_ , _0_ , _____ , _____ , _____ , _____

6. Complete the number sequence below by skip counting by 25s.

a) 75, 100, _____, _____, _____

b) 375, 400, _____, _____, _____

c) 125, 150, _____, _____, _____

d) 600, 625, _____, _____, _____

e) 200, 225, _____, _____, _____

f) 850, 875, _____, _____, _____

1. Count by 5s.

    ___5___, _____, _____, _____, _____, _____, _____, _____, _____

    _____, _____, _____, _____, _____, _____, _____, _____, _____

2. Count on by 5s.

    a) 65, _____, _____, _____

    b) 105, _____, _____, _____

    c) 245, _____, _____, _____

    d) 315, _____, _____, _____

    e) 560, _____, _____, _____

    f) 785, _____, _____, _____

3. The numbers below are the numbers you say counting by 3s.
   Use the pattern in the first two rows to fill in the missing numbers.

    ___3___, ___6___, ___9___, ___12___, ___15___, ___18___, ___21___, ___24___, ___27___, ___30___,

    ___33___, ___36___, ___39___, ___42___, ___45___, _____, ___51___, _____, _____, ___60___,

    _____, ___66___, _____, _____, _____, _____, _____, _____, _____, _____,

    _____, _____, _____

4. Hien counted by 2s, 3s or 5s.
   Fill in the missing numbers and say what he counted by.

    a)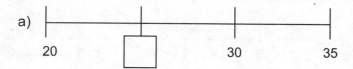

    He counted by _____.

    b)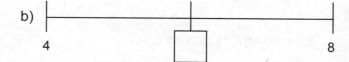

    He counted by _____.

    c)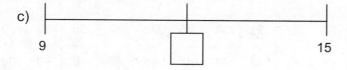

    He counted by _____.

    d)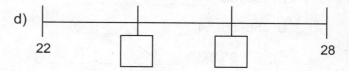

    He counted by _____.

    e)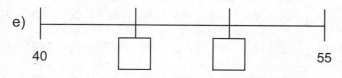

    He counted by _____.

    f)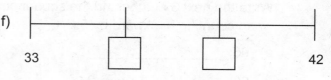

    He counted by _____.

5. Explain how you found your answer to Question 4 e).

 jump math
MULTIPLYING POTENTIAL.

Number Sense 1

NS3-15: Counting Backward by 2s and 5s

1. Circle the numbers that you would say when counting backward by 2s starting at 52.

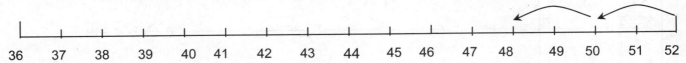

36 37 38 39 40 41 42 43 44 45 46 47 48 49 50 51 52

Record all the circled numbers here: __52 , 50 , 48_____

2. Circle the numbers that you would say when counting backward by 5s starting at 80.

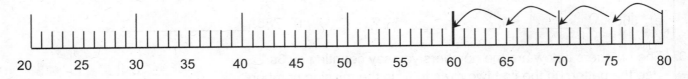

20   25   30   35   40   45   50   55   60   65   70   75   80

Record all the circled numbers here: _____

3. Circle the numbers that you would say when counting backward by 10s starting at 90.

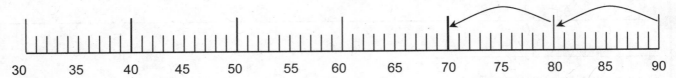

30   35   40   45   50   55   60   65   70   75   80   85   90

Record all the circled numbers here: _____

4. Using the hundreds chart ...

   Write the next 3 numbers in the sequences when counting backward by 2s.

   a) 35, 33, 31, _____, _____, _____

   b) 58, 56, 54, _____, _____, _____

   c) 97, 95, 93, _____, _____, _____

   d) 79, 77, 75, _____, _____, _____

   Write the next 3 numbers in the sequences when counting backward by 5s.

   e) 95, _____, _____, _____

   f) 60, _____, _____, _____

   g) 35, _____, _____, _____

   h) 75, _____, _____, _____

1	2	3	4	5	6	7	8	9	10
11	12	13	14	15	16	17	18	19	20
21	22	23	24	25	26	27	28	29	30
31	32	33	34	35	36	37	38	39	40
41	42	43	44	45	46	47	48	49	50
51	52	53	54	55	56	57	58	59	60
61	62	63	64	65	66	67	68	69	70
71	72	73	74	75	76	77	78	79	80
81	82	83	84	85	86	87	88	89	90
91	92	93	94	95	96	97	98	99	100

1. Count by 10s to continue the pattern.

    a) 10, 20, 30, _____, _____, _____

    b) 40, 50, 60, _____, _____, _____

    c) 70, 80, 90, _____, _____, _____

    d) 200, 210, 220, _____, _____, _____

    e) 440, 450, 460, _____, _____, _____

    f) 240, 250, 260, _____, _____, _____

    g) 170, 180, 190, _____, _____, _____

    h) 330, 340, 350, _____, _____, _____

    i) 360, 370, 380, _____, _____, _____

    j) 680, 690, 700, _____, _____, _____

2. Kara estimates that there are about 10 jelly beans in a jar.

    a) About how many jelly beans are in 2 jars? _____

    b) About how many jelly beans are in 4 jars? _____

3. Count by 10s and join the points to create a shape.

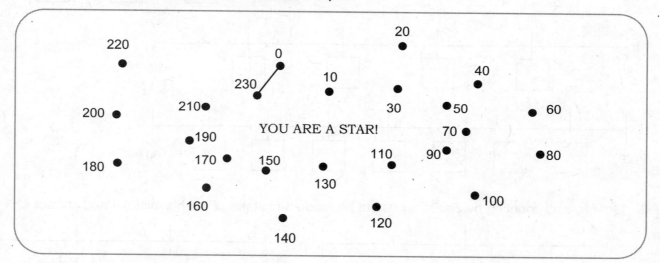

YOU ARE A STAR!

4. Count by 10s to complete the pattern. The first one has been done for you.

    a) 47, 57, 67, __77__, __87__, __97__

    **NOTE: The ones digit stays the same, and
    the number of tens increases by 1 each time.**

    b) 48, 58, 68, _____, _____, _____

    c) 25, 35, 45, _____, _____, _____

    e) 57, 67, 77, _____, _____, _____

    d) 36, 46, 56, _____, _____, _____

    g) 161, 171, 181, _____, _____, _____

    f) 72, 82, 92, _____, _____, _____

5. Write the next 3 numbers when counting backward by 10s.

    a) 80, _____, _____, _____

    b) 70, _____, _____, _____

    c) 50, _____, _____, _____

    d) 100, _____, _____, _____

1. Continue the pattern counting by 4s.

<u>4</u> , <u>8</u> , <u>12</u> , <u>16</u> , <u>20</u> ,

<u>24</u> , <u>28</u> , <u>32</u> , <u>36</u> , <u>40</u> ,

_____ , _____ , <u>52</u> , _____ , _____ ,

_____ , _____ , _____ , _____ , _____

2. Karla counted by 2s, 3s, 4s, 5s, or 10s.
   Fill in the missing numbers.

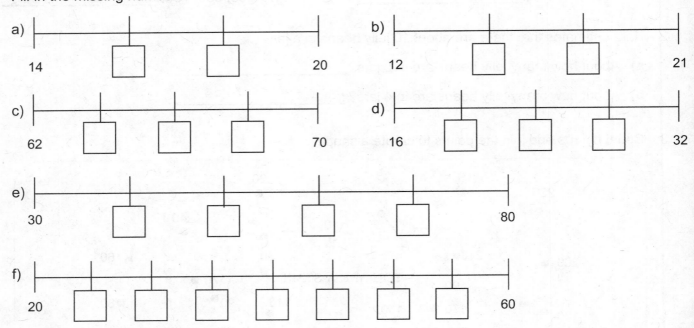

a) 14 ____ ____ 20

b) 12 ____ ____ 21

c) 62 ____ ____ ____ 70

d) 16 ____ ____ ____ 32

e) 30 ____ ____ ____ ____ 80

f) 20 ____ ____ ____ ____ ____ ____ ____ 60

3. George was counting by 2s, 3s, or 5s but he made a mistake. Find his mistake and correct it.

a) 20 [24] 30

b) 50 [55] [61] 65

c) 84 [86] [87] 90

d) 32 [34] [38] 41

4. Skip count to find out how many hops it would take to travel 5 metres.

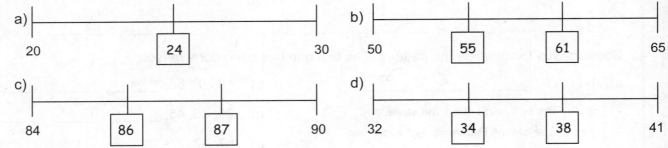

a) 0 m — 1 m

b) 0 m — 1 m

c) 0 m — 1 m

5. Describe any patterns you see in the array in Question 1.

1. Count by 100s to continue the pattern.

   a) 100, 200, 300, _____, _____, _____

   b) 300, 400, 500, _____, _____, _____

   c) 400, 500, 600, _____, _____, _____

   d) 600, 700, 800, _____, _____, _____

2. There are 200 marbles in a bag. How many marbles would there be in …

   a) 2 bags? _____

   b) 3 bags? _____

   c) 4 bags? _____

3.

   Can you estimate how many bikes are parked at the station if each lot holds approximately 100 bikes?

Lot 1	Lot 3	TRAIN STATION		Lot 7
Lot 2	Lot 4	Lot 5	Lot 6	Lot 8

   _____

4. Each beehive at a farm has approximately 100 bees inside.

   Can you estimate how many bees would be inside …

   a) 2 beehives? _____

   b) 7 beehives? _____

   c) 3 beehives? _____

   d) 8 beehives? _____

   e) 9 beehives? _____

   f) 10 beehives? _____

5. Complete the pattern.

   a) 1200, 1300, 1400, 1_____, 1_____

   b) 1500, 1600, 1700, _____, _____

   c) 600, 700, 800, _____, _____

   d) 3300, 3400, 3500, _____, _____

BONUS

6. Count down by 100s.

   a) 600, 500, 400, _____, _____, _____

   b) 900, 800, 700, _____, _____, _____

7. Count by 100s to complete the pattern. The first one has been done for you.

   a) 157, 257, 357, __457__, __557__, __657__

   b) 254, 354, 454, _____, _____, _____

   NOTE: The ones and tens digits stay the same, and the number of hundreds increases by 1.

   c) 313, 413, 513, _____, _____, _____

   d) 136, 236, 336, _____, _____, _____

   e) 182, 282, 382, _____, _____, _____

   f) 419, 519, 619, _____, _____, _____

   g) 438, 538, 638, _____, _____, _____

NS3-19: Regrouping

Selma has 2 tens blocks and 12 ones blocks. She regroups 10 ones blocks as 1 tens block.

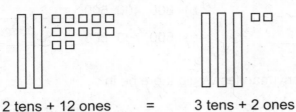

2 tens + 12 ones   =   3 tens + 2 ones

----

1. Regroup each group of 10 ones as 1 tens block.

a)
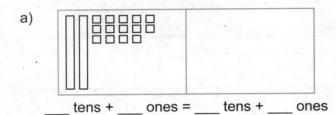

___ tens + ___ ones = ___ tens + ___ ones

b)
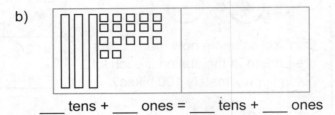

___ tens + ___ ones = ___ tens + ___ ones

c)
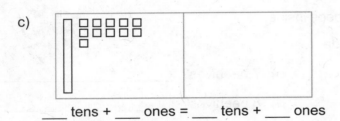

___ tens + ___ ones = ___ tens + ___ ones

d)
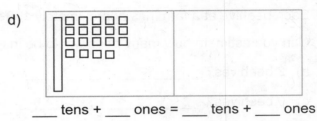

___ tens + ___ ones = ___ tens + ___ ones

e)
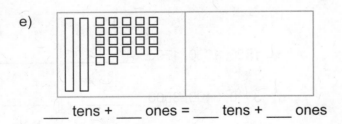

___ tens + ___ ones = ___ tens + ___ ones

f)
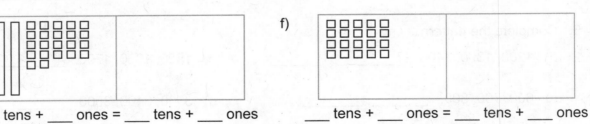

___ tens + ___ ones = ___ tens + ___ ones

2. Complete the charts by regrouping 10 ones as 1 ten. The first one has been done for you.

a)

tens	ones
4	13
4 + 1 = 5	3

b)

tens	ones
6	14

c)

tens	ones
8	15

d)

tens	ones
2	19

e)

tens	ones
6	17

f)

tens	ones
1	18

3. There are 10 dots in each row.
   Count by 10s to find out how many ones there are.
   Then write how many tens there are.

a)

___30__ ones = _____ tens

b)

_____ ones = _____ tens

c)

_____ ones = _____ tens

d)

_____ ones = _____ tens

e)

_____ ones = _____ ten

f)

_____ ones = _____ tens

4. Count by 10s, then continue counting by 1s to find out how many dots there are. Then write how many tens and ones there are.

a)

_____ ones = ___ tens + ___ ones

b)

_____ ones = ___ tens + ___ ones

c)

_____ ones = ___ tens + ___ ones

d)

_____ ones = ___ tens + ___ one

e)

_____ ones = ___ ten + ___ ones

f)

_____ ones = ___ ten + ___ ones

5. Regroup the ones as tens. The first one has been done for you.

a) 68 ones = ___6__ tens + ___8__ ones

b) 42 ones = _____ tens + _____ ones

c) 93 ones = _____ tens + _____ ones

d) 35 ones = _____ tens + _____ ones

e) 17 ones = _____ ten + _____ ones

f) 84 ones = _____ tens + _____ ones

g) 8 ones = _____ tens + _____ ones

h) 30 ones = _____ tens + _____ ones

NS3-20: Regrouping (Advanced)

Paul has 3 hundreds blocks, 12 tens blocks, and 3 ones blocks.
He regroups 10 tens blocks as 1 hundreds block.

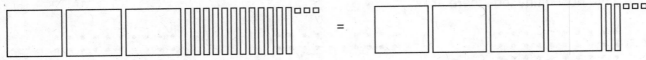

3 hundreds + 12 tens + 3 ones   4 hundreds + 2 tens + 3 ones

----

1. Regroup 10 tens as 1 hundred, or 10 ones as 1 ten.

    a) 4 hundreds + 15 tens + 6 ones = _____ hundreds + _____ tens + _____ ones

    b) 3 hundreds + 14 tens + 2 ones = _____ hundreds + _____ tens + _____ ones

    c) 6 hundreds + 19 tens + 3 ones = _____ hundreds + _____ tens + _____ ones

    d) 6 hundreds + 3 tens + 15 ones = _____ hundreds + _____ tens + _____ ones

    e) 9 hundreds + 8 tens + 16 ones = _____

    _____

2. Regroup as many pennies for dimes as you can.
    REMEMBER: 10 pennies = 1 dime; 20 pennies = 2 dimes; 30 pennies = 3 dimes, etc.)

    a)
dimes	pennies
3	27
3 + 2	7
5	7

    b)
dimes	pennies
5	23

    c)
dimes	pennies
4	37

    d)
dimes	pennies
2	32

    Regroup 20 pennies as 2 dimes:

3. Write the money amounts using the fewest possible number of coins. The first one is done for you.

    a)
	dollars	dimes	pennies
	4	34	27
Step 1	4	34 + 2 = 36	7
Step 2	4 + 3 = 7	6	7

    b)
dollars	dimes	pennies
2	37	21

    c)
dollars	dimes	pennies
3	56	28

    d)
dollars	dimes	pennies
1	31	68

1. Find the <u>sum</u> of the numbers below by drawing a picture and by adding the digits. Don't worry about drawing the model in too much detail.

a) **24 + 32**

with base ten materials		with numerals	
tens	ones	tens	ones
24		2	4
32		3	2
sum		5	6

b) **13 + 22**

with base ten materials		with numerals	
tens	ones	tens	ones
13			
22			
sum			

c) **23 + 33**

with base ten materials		with numerals	
tens	ones	tens	ones
23			
33			
sum			

d) **21 + 22**

with base ten materials		with numerals	
tens	ones	tens	ones
21			
22			
sum			

2. Add the numbers by adding the digits.

a) 2 1
  + 2 3

b) 1 3
  + 2 2

c) 4 1
  + 2 2

d) 1 2
  + 4 5

e) 5 2
  + 3 2

f) 2 4
  + 3 1

g) 1 2
  + 1 5

h) 2 1
  + 3 1

i) 4 2
  + 1 3

j) 3 1
  + 2 2

NS3-22: Adding with Regrouping (or Carrying)

1. Add the numbers below by drawing a picture and by adding the digits.
   Use base ten materials to show how to combine the numbers and how to regroup.

a) 25 + 17

	with base ten materials		with numerals	
	tens	one	tens	one
25			2	5
17			1	7
sum			3	12
		exchange 10 ones for 1 ten		
		after regrouping	4	2

b) 33 + 29

	with base ten materials		with numerals	
	tens	one	tens	one
33				
29				
sum				

c) 14 + 58

	with base ten materials		with numerals	
	tens	one	tens	one
14				
58				
sum				

d) 19 + 5

	with base ten materials		with numerals	
	tens	one	tens	one
19				
5				
sum				

2. Add the numbers by regrouping.

Step 1:   Regroup 10 ones as 1 ten.

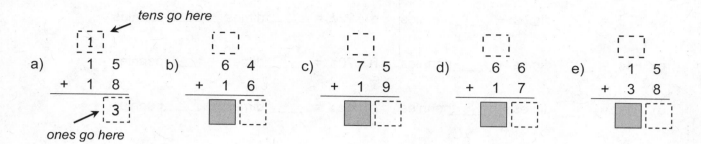

tens go here

a)
```
    1
    1 5
  + 1 8
  ─────
    3
```
ones go here

b)
```
  ┌─┐
  └─┘
    6 4
  + 1 6
  ─────
  ▨ ┌─┐
```

c)
```
  ┌─┐
  └─┘
    7 5
  + 1 9
  ─────
  ▨ ┌─┐
```

d)
```
  ┌─┐
  └─┘
    6 6
  + 1 7
  ─────
  ▨ ┌─┐
```

e)
```
  ┌─┐
  └─┘
    1 5
  + 3 8
  ─────
  ▨ ┌─┐
```

f)
```
    1
    1 3
  + 1 9
  ─────
  ▨ ☐
```

g)
```
  ┌─┐
  └─┘
    2 4
  + 3 8
  ─────
  ▨ ┌─┐
```

h)
```
  ┌─┐
  └─┘
    5 4
  + 1 8
  ─────
  ▨ ┌─┐
```

i)
```
  ┌─┐
  └─┘
    2 7
  + 6 9
  ─────
  ▨ ┌─┐
```

j)
```
  ┌─┐
  └─┘
    4 6
  + 4 8
  ─────
  ▨ ┌─┐
```

Step 2:   Add the numbers in the tens column.

k)
```
    1
    1 2
  + 1 8
  ─────
    3 0
```

l)
```
    1
    1 3
  + 1 7
  ─────
    ┌─┐ 0
```

m)
```
    1
    1 5
  + 2 8
  ─────
    ┌─┐ 3
```

n)
```
    1
    2 6
  + 2 6
  ─────
    ┌─┐ 2
```

o)
```
    1
    3 8
  + 2 7
  ─────
    ┌─┐ 5
```

3. Add the numbers by regrouping (or carrying).

a)
```
    1
    2 5
  + 1 7
  ─────
    4 2
```

b)
```
    2 6
  + 1 6
  ─────
```

c)
```
    3 8
  + 1 4
  ─────
```

d)
```
    2 8
  + 2 3
  ─────
```

e)
```
    4 6
  + 2 5
  ─────
```

f)
```
    4 9
  + 1 4
  ─────
```

g)
```
    3 9
  + 4 6
  ─────
```

h)
```
    2 8
  + 1 7
  ─────
```

i)
```
    1 6
  + 2 8
  ─────
```

j)
```
    4 8
  + 2 8
  ─────
```

NS3-23: Adding with Money

1. Rewrite each money amount in dimes and pennies.

   a) 51¢ = __5__ dimes + __1__ penny   b) 23¢ = _____ dimes + _____ pennies

   c) 67¢ = _____ dimes + _____ pennies   d) 92¢ = _____ dimes + _____ pennies

   e) 84¢ = _____ dimes + _____ pennies   f) 70¢ = _____ dimes + _____ pennies

   g) 2¢ = _____ dimes + _____ pennies   h) 5¢ = _____ dimes + _____ pennies

2. Show how to regroup ten pennies as 1 dime.

   a)

dimes	pennies
2	12
3	2

   After regrouping

   b)

dimes	pennies
5	13

   c)

dimes	pennies
7	17

   d)

dimes	pennies
4	18

3. Find the total number of dimes and pennies. Then regroup.

   a)

dimes	pennies
3	5
2	6
5	11
6	1

   Total after regrouping {

   b)

dimes	pennies
2	6
3	6

   c)

dimes	pennies
5	2
2	9

   d)

dimes	pennies
3	3
4	9

4. Add by regrouping 10 pennies as 1 dime.

   a)   3 7 ¢
      + 2 5 ¢
      _____
          ¢

   b)   2 3 ¢
      + 4 9 ¢
      _____
          ¢

   c)   2 6 ¢
      + 3 7 ¢
      _____
          ¢

   d)   4 7 ¢
      + 6 7 ¢
      _____
          ¢

   e)   2 8 ¢
      + 4 8 ¢
      _____
          ¢

5. Add by lining the dimes and pennies up in the grid.

   a) 15¢ + 17¢   b) 23¢ + 27¢   c) 48¢ + 59¢   d) 26¢ + 34¢   e) 27¢ + 85¢

	1	5	¢																
+	1	7	¢																

Marzuk adds 142 + 275 using base ten materials.

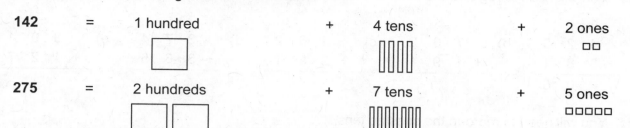

| **142** | = | 1 hundred | + | 4 tens | + | 2 ones |
| **+ 275** | = | 2 hundreds | + | 7 tens | + | 5 ones |

| = | 3 hundreds | + | 11 tens | + | 7 ones |

Then, to get the final answer, Marzuk regroup 10 tens as 1 hundred.

| = | 4 hundreds | + | 1 ten | + | 7 ones |

----

1. Add the numbers using base ten materials or a picture (and record your work below).

a)
$$242 = \underline{\quad 2 \quad} \text{ hundreds} + \underline{\quad 4 \quad} \text{ tens} + \underline{\quad 2 \quad} \text{ ones}$$
$$+ 384 = \underline{\quad 3 \quad} \text{ hundreds} + \underline{\quad 8 \quad} \text{ tens} + \underline{\quad 4 \quad} \text{ ones}$$
$$= \underline{\quad 5 \quad} \text{ hundreds} + \underline{\quad 12 \quad} \text{ tens} + \underline{\quad 6 \quad} \text{ ones}$$
after regrouping $= \underline{\quad 6 \quad} \text{ hundreds} + \underline{\quad 2 \quad} \text{ tens} + \underline{\quad 6 \quad} \text{ ones}$

b)
$$394 = \underline{\qquad} \text{ hundreds} + \underline{\qquad} \text{ tens} + \underline{\qquad} \text{ ones}$$
$$+ 531 = \underline{\qquad} \text{ hundreds} + \underline{\qquad} \text{ tens} + \underline{\qquad} \text{ one}$$
$$= \underline{\qquad} \text{ hundreds} + \underline{\qquad} \text{ tens} + \underline{\qquad} \text{ ones}$$
after regrouping $= \underline{\qquad} \text{ hundreds} + \underline{\qquad} \text{ tens} + \underline{\qquad} \text{ ones}$

c)
$$156 = \underline{\qquad} \text{ hundred} + \underline{\qquad} \text{ tens} + \underline{\qquad} \text{ ones}$$
$$+ 483 = \underline{\qquad} \text{ hundreds} + \underline{\qquad} \text{ tens} + \underline{\qquad} \text{ ones}$$
$$= \underline{\qquad} \text{ hundreds} + \underline{\qquad} \text{ tens} + \underline{\qquad} \text{ ones}$$
after regrouping $= \underline{\qquad} \text{ hundreds} + \underline{\qquad} \text{ tens} + \underline{\qquad} \text{ ones}$

2. Add. You will need to regroup the tens. The first one is started for you.

a)
```
  [1]
    4 2 5
  + 3 8 1
  ───────
      0 6
```
b)
```
    [ ]
    7 3 2
  + 1 9 1
  ───────
```
c)
```
    [ ]
    4 6 2
  + 2 5 1
  ───────
```
d)
```
    3 7 4
  + 3 6 5
  ───────
```
e)
```
    3 9 1
  + 1 2 7
  ───────
```

3. Add. You will need to regroup the ones as tens.

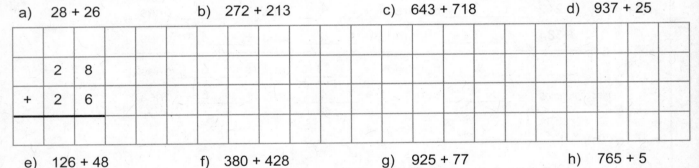

a)
```
    [ ]
    4 5 6
  +   2 9
  ───────
```
b)
```
    [ ]
    1 7 5
  + 4 1 8
  ───────
```
c)
```
    [ ]
    6 1 4
  +   5 7
  ───────
```
d)
```
    2 3 8
  + 3 4 5
  ───────
```
e)
```
    7 2 7
  + 5 3 8
  ───────
```

4. Add, regrouping where necessary.

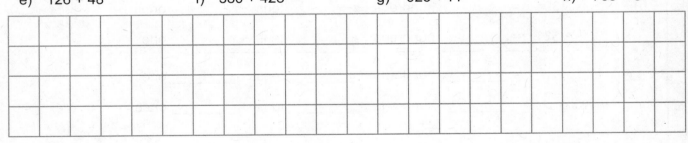

a)
```
    4 2 1
  + 2 9 3
  ───────
```
b)
```
    2 6 3
  + 3 7 2
  ───────
```
c)
```
    2 4 3
  + 5 1 6
  ───────
```
d)
```
    4 2 8
  + 3 6 7
  ───────
```
e)
```
    6 2 7
  + 2 3 1
  ───────
```
f)
```
    7 3 5
  + 1 8 7
  ───────
```

5. Add by lining the numbers up correctly in the grid. The first one has been started for you.

a) 28 + 26   b) 272 + 213   c) 643 + 718   d) 937 + 25

	2	8														
+	2	6														

e) 126 + 48   f) 380 + 428   g) 925 + 77   h) 765 + 5

BONUS

6. How do you think you might add the following numbers? Write what you think the answer might be.

a)
```
    2 3 5 1
  + 5 1 3 4
  ─────────
```
b)
```
    3 5 8 1
  + 4 3 1 7
  ─────────
```
c)
```
    3 8 9 5
  + 2 0 1 3
  ─────────
```
d)
```
    4 5 1 2 3
  + 5 4 1 7 5
  ───────────
```

Nevina subtracts 37 – 24 using base ten materials. She makes a model of 37. Then she takes away 2 tens and 4 ones (because 24 = 2 tens + 4 ones).

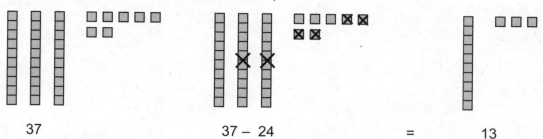

37   37 – 24   =   13

----

1. Perform the subtractions by crossing out tens blocks and ones blocks. Draw your final answer in the right-hand box. The first one has been done for you.

a)

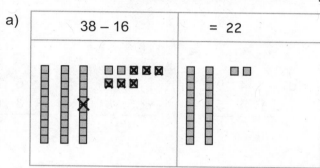

| 38 – 16 | = 22 |

b)

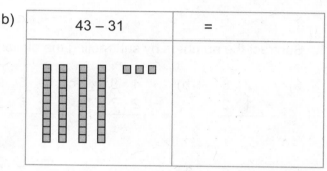

| 43 – 31 | = |

c)

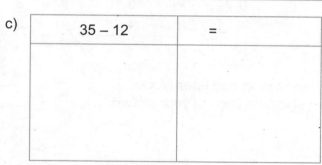

| 35 – 12 | = |

d)

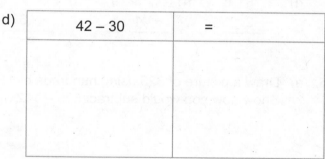

| 42 – 30 | = |

2. Write the number of tens and ones in each number. Then subtract the number.

a)   39 = 3 tens + 9 ones

   – 25 = 2 tens + 5 ones
   _____

       = 1 ten + 4 ones

       = 14

b)   68 = ____ tens + ____ ones

   – 42 = ____ tens + ____ ones
   _____

       = ____ tens + ____ ones

       = _____

c)   67 = ____ tens + ____ ones

   – 33 = ____ tens + ____ ones
   _____

       = ____ tens + ____ ones

       = _____

d)   96 = ____ tens + ____ ones

   – 62 = ____ tens + ____ ones
   _____

       = ____ tens + ____ ones

       = _____

NS3-25: Subtracting 2- and 3-Digit Numbers (continued)

3. Subtract by writing the number of tens and ones in each number.

a) $46 = 40 + 6$

   $-\ 32 = 30 + 2$
   _____

   $\quad\quad = 10 + 4$

   $\quad\quad = 14$

b) $95 =$

   $-\ 62 =$
   _____

   $\quad\quad =$

   $\quad\quad =$

c) $37 =$

   $-\ 11 =$
   _____

   $\quad\quad =$

   $\quad\quad =$

d) $63 =$

   $-\ 20 =$
   _____

e) $29 =$

   $-\ 4 =$
   _____

f) $58 =$

   $-\ 41 =$
   _____

4. Subtract the numbers by subtracting the digits.

a)
```
  2 8
- 1 2
_____
```

b)
```
  4 8
- 2 7
_____
```

c)
```
  6 9
- 5 3
_____
```

d)
```
  4 9
- 4 5
_____
```

e)
```
  8 7
- 5 3
_____
```

f)
```
  6 2
- 3 0
_____
```

g)
```
  5 6
- 2 1
_____
```

h)
```
  3 9
- 1 5
_____
```

i)
```
  7 2
- 6 0
_____
```

j)
```
  6 2
- 4 1
_____
```

k)
```
  9 6
- 4 3
_____
```

l)
```
  8 7
- 3 4
_____
```

5. a) Draw a picture of 325 using hundreds blocks, tens blocks and ones blocks.
    Show how you would subtract 325 – 112 by crossing out parts of your picture.

   b) Now subtract the numbers by lining up the digits and subtracting. Do you get the same answer?

BONUS
6. Subtract.

a)
```
  7 2 9
- 3 1 6
_____
```

b)
```
  8 9 5
- 2 5 4
_____
```

c)
```
  5 2 4
- 4 0 1
_____
```

d)
```
  3 9 8
- 1 6 3
_____
```

e)
```
  5 9 2
- 1 7 0
_____
```

NS3-26: Subtracting by Regrouping

Rina subtracts 34 − 19 using base ten materials.

Step 1:
Rina represents 34 using base ten materials …

Step 2:
9 (the ones digit of 19) is greater than 4 (the ones digit of 34) so Rina regroups 1 ten as 10 ones …

Step 3:
Rina subtracts 19 (she takes away 1 tens block and 9 ones) …

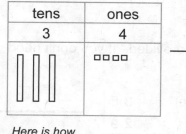

Here is how Rina uses numerals to show her work:

```
  3 4
− 1 9
```

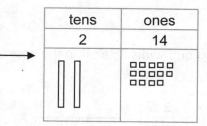

Here is how Rina shows the regrouping:

```
  2 14
  3̶ 4̶
− 1 9
```

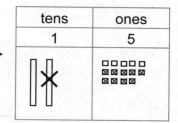

And now Rina can subtract 14 − 9 ones and 2 − 1 tens:

```
  2 14
  3̶ 4̶
− 1 9
  1 5
```

- -

1. In these questions, Rina doesn't have enough ones to subtract. Help her by regrouping 1 tens block as 10 ones. Show how she would rewrite her subtraction statement.

a) 33 − 18

tens	ones
3	3

	3	3
−	1	8

tens	ones
2	13

	2	13
	3̶	3̶
−	1	8

b) 54 − 28

tens	ones
5	4

	5	4
−	2	8

tens	ones

	5̶	4̶
−	2	8

c) 32 − 17

tens	ones
3	2

	3	2
−	1	7

tens	ones

	3	2
−	1	7

d) 23 − 19

tens	ones
2	3

	2	3
−	1	9

tens	ones

	2	3
−	1	9

NS3-26: Subtracting by Regrouping *(continued)*

2. Subtract by regrouping.

a)

	2	11
	~~3~~	~~1~~
−	1	9
	1	2

b)

	4	4
−	2	8

c)

	5	3
−	3	6

d)

	6	2
−	1	5

e)

	8	5
−		8

3. For the questions where you need to regroup, write "Help!" in the space provided. If you don't need to regroup, write "OK."

a)
```
    2 3
  - 1 7
```
Help!
3 is less than 7

b)
```
    3 5
  - 1 3
```
OK

c)
```
    8 5
  - 2 9
```
_____

d)
```
    2 2
  - 1 7
```
_____

e)
```
    8 5
  - 1 7
```
_____

f)
```
    2 2
  - 1 9
```
_____

g)
```
    8 1
  - 6 7
```
_____

h)
```
    8 8
  - 3 4
```
_____

i)
```
    2 7
  - 1 6
```
_____

j)
```
    3 4
  - 1 5
```
_____

k)
```
    8 5
  - 6 7
```
_____

l)
```
    7 5
  - 3 9
```
_____

m)
```
    2 1
  - 1 7
```
_____

n)
```
    3 2
  - 1 8
```
_____

o)
```
    2 1
  -   8
```
_____

p)
```
    6 7
  - 2 9
```
_____

q)
```
    4 7
  - 2 3
```
_____

r)
```
    5 7
  - 3 2
```
_____

4. Go back and finish the subtraction questions above.

To subtract 325 −172, Samir regroups 1 hundreds block as 10 tens blocks.

hundreds	tens	ones
3	2	5

hundreds	tens	ones
2	12	5

hundreds	tens	ones
1	5	3

```
   3 2 5
 - 1 7 2
```

```
   2 12
   3̷ 2̷ 5
 - 1 7 2
```

```
   2 12
   3̷ 2̷ 5
 - 1 7 2
 ───────
   1 5 3
```

---

1. Subtract by regrouping the **hundreds**. The first one has been started for you.

a)
```
   3  12
   4̷  2̷  7
 - 2  9  2
```

b)
```
   5  3  8
 - 2  9  5
```

c)
```
   3  1  7
 - 1  8  6
```

d)
```
   9  4  2
 - 5  7  0
```

2. Subtract by regrouping the **tens**: The first one has been started for you.

a)
```
      2  13
   8  3̷  3̷
 - 3  1  9
```

b)
```
   5  8  3
 - 2  7  7
```

c)
```
   9  6  3
 - 4  1  7
```

d)
```
   4  5  0
 - 1  3  6
```

3. For the questions below, you will have to regroup **twice**.

Example:

Step 1:
```
   2  11
   5  3̷  1̷
 - 2  7  9
```

Step 2:
```
   2  11
   5̷  3̷  1̷
 - 2  7  9
 ──────────
         2
```

Step 3:
```
      12
   4  2̷  11
   5̷  3̷  1̷
 - 2  7  9
 ──────────
         2
```

Step 4:
```
      12
   4  2̷  11
   5̷  3̷  1̷
 - 2  7  9
 ──────────
      5  2
```

Step 5:
```
      12
   4  2̷  11
   5̷  3̷  1̷
 - 2  7  9
 ──────────
   2  5  2
```

a)
```
   5  3  2
 - 2  9  8
```

b)
```
   3  1  2
 - 1  8  6
```

c)
```
   8  2  3
 - 2  7  9
```

d)
```
   1  0  0
 -    5  7
```

NS3-28: Mental Math

1. Show all the ways you can decompose the number.

   a) 7 = ☐1 + ☐
      ☐2 + ☐
      ☐3 + ☐

   b) 4 = ☐1 + ☐
      ☐2 + ☐

   c) 6 = ☐ + ☐
      ☐ + ☐
      ☐ + ☐

2. Show all the ways you can decompose 10.

   10 = ☐ + ☐
        ☐ + ☐
        ☐ + ☐
        ☐ + ☐
        ☐ + ☐

3. Circle the pair that adds to 10.

   a) ②   7   ⑧

   b) 3   7   4

   c) 5   3   5

   d) 6   4   5

   e) 1   8   9

4. Find the pair that adds to 10. Rewrite the addition statement.

   a) 4 + 5 + 6 = 10 + ☐5

   b) 7 + 3 + 4 = 10 + ☐

   c) 8 + 3 + 2 = 10 + ☐

   d) 6 + 9 + 4 = 10 + ☐

   e) 9 + 1 + 7 = 10 + ☐

   f) 5 + 8 + 2 = 10 + ☐

5. Use the pattern in a) b) and c) below to add.

   a) 10 + 5 = ___15___

   b) 10 + 7 = ___17___

   c) 40 + 8 = ___48___

   d) 50 + 9 = _____

   e) 60 + 1 = _____

   f) 20 + 3 = _____

   g) 40 + 4 = _____

   h) 30 + 6 = _____

   i) 90 + 8 = _____

   j) 90 + 7 = _____

   k) 120 + 5 = _____

   l) 160 + 4 = _____

6. Fill in the boxes.

a) 8 + 6 = 8 + [2] + [4]

   these make 10   left over

b) 9 + 5 = 9 + [ ] + [ ]

   these make 10   left over

c) 6 + 5 = 6 + [ ] + [ ]

d) 5 + 7 = 5 + [ ] + [ ]

e) 9 + 4 = 9 + [ ] + [ ]

f) 8 + 8 = 8 + [ ] + [ ]

g) 7 + 6 = 7 + [ ] + [ ]

h) 9 + 6 = 9 + [ ] + [ ]

7. Add by following the steps.

a) 7 + 5 = [7] + [3] + [2] = 10 + 2 = 12

   these make 10   left over

b) 26 + 5 = 26 + [ ] + [ ] = _____

   these make 30   left over

c) 78 + 6 = 78 + [ ] + [ ] = _____

   these make 80   left over

d) 45 + 8 = 45 + [ ] + [ ] = _____

   these make 50   left over

8. Find the answers mentally.

a) Roger has saved $38.
   His parents gave him $7.
   How much money does Roger have?

   _____

b) Damon has 26 stickers.
   Chloe has 7 stickers.
   How many do they have altogether?

   _____

9. Explain how you would add 37 + 5 mentally.

NS3-29: Parts and Totals

1. Shade boxes to show the number of marbles. Then find …

- the total number of marbles
- the difference between the number of green and blue marbles

a) 5 green marbles
   3 blue marbles

difference: _____2 marbles_____

green

blue

total: _____8 marbles_____

b) 4 green marbles
   6 blue marbles

difference: _____

green

blue

total: _____

c) 8 green marbles
   4 blue marbles

difference: _____

green

blue

total: _____

BONUS

d) 5 green marbles
   2 more green marbles than blue marbles

difference: _____

green

blue

total: _____

e) 3 green marbles
   _____ blue marbles

difference: _____

green

blue

total: _____4 marbles_____

2. Follow the steps in Question 1.
    Put the colour of marble that you have more of on top.

a) 4 green marbles
    5 blue marbles

difference: _____

_____blue_____

_____green_____

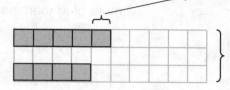

} total: _____

b) 3 green marbles
    7 blue marbles

difference: _____

_____

_____

} total: _____

c) 9 green marbles
    5 blue marbles

difference: _____

_____

_____

} total: _____

d) ___ blue marbles
    2 green marbles

difference: _____

_____

_____

} total: ____ 6 marbles ____

e) 3 green marbles
    4 more blue marbles than green

difference: _____

_____

_____

} total: _____

3. Draw a picture (as in Question 1) and make a chart for each question.

a) 3 green marbles
    2 more blue marbles than
    green marbles

b) 11 marbles in total
    6 green marbles

c) 12 marbles in total
    7 blue marbles

NS3-30: Parts and Totals (Advanced)

1. Write the missing numbers.

Green Marbles	Blue Marbles	Total Number of Marbles	How many more marbles of one colour than the other?
3	5	8	2 more blue marbles than green
4		6	
	2	3	
3			1 more blue marble than green
	2		1 more green marble than blue
	4		1 more blue marble than green

2. The fact family for the addition statement **2 + 4 = 6** is: **4 + 2 = 6**; **6 − 4 = 2** and **6 − 2 = 4**.

   Write the fact family of equations for the following statements:

   a) 3 + 4 = 7 _____

   b) 5 + 4 = 9 _____

3. Fill in the chart.

	Green Marbles	Purple Marbles	Total Number of Marbles	Fact Family	How many more marbles of one color than the other?
a)	7	2	9	9 − 2 = 7 7 + 2 = 9 9 − 7 = 2 2 + 7 = 9	5 more green than purple
b)	6		10		
c)	2	9			
d)		5			4 more green than purple

4. Use the correct symbol (**+** or **−**).

a) Number of green marbles ☐ Number of blue marbles = Total number of marbles

b) Number of green marbles ☐ Number of blue marbles = How many more green marbles than blue marbles?

c) Number of green apples ☐ Number of red apples = Total number of apples

d) Number of green grapes ☐ Number of purple grapes = How many more green grapes than purple grapes?

e) Number of yellow beans ☐ Number of green beans = How many more yellow beans?

f) Number of red marbles ☐ Number of blue marbles = How many more red marbles?

5. Draw pictures on grid paper (as in Question 1 in "Parts and Totals") for each question.

a) Kate has 3 green fish and 4 yellow fish. How many fish does she have?

b) Ed has 5 green marbles. He has 3 more green marbles than blue marbles. How many marbles does he have?

c) Serge has 5 pets. 3 are cats. The rest are dogs. How many dogs does he have?

d) Leesa walked 4 km. Mark walked 3 km. How much further did Leesa walk?

Answer the remaining questions in your notebook.

1. Ken has $7 and Reg has $15.
   How much money do they have altogether?

2. Anne is 12 years old. Her sister is 23.
   How much older is her sister?

3. A school library has 520 books.
   150 were borrowed.
   How many books are left?

4. 52 children went on a school trip.
   27 of the children were girls.
   How many were boys?

5. Leslie paid 75¢ for a pen that cost 49¢.
   How much change did he get back?

6. Shelly has 57¢. Gerome has 42¢.
   How much more money does Shelly have?

7. Alice's mother is 47. Her aunt is 33.
   How much older is Alice's mother than
   Alice's aunt?

8. Sam sold 27 raffle tickets in two days.
   On Thursday, he sold 13 tickets.
   How many tickets did he sell on
   Wednesday?

9. Midori had 35 pencil crayons.
   She lost 4.
   How many does she have left?

10. Imogen read 2 books by Roald Dahl.
    The BFG is 208 pages long.
    Charlie and the Chocolate Factory
    is 155 pages long.
    How many pages did she read altogether?

11. A single woolly mammoth skull weighs
    110 kg. How much would
    2 skulls weigh?

12. Calvin explored 2 caves in the Rocky
    Mountains from end to end. Wapiabi
    Cave is 540 metres long and Serendipity
    Cave is 470 metres long. How far did
    Calvin travel in the caves altogether?

NS3-32: Larger Numbers

1. Write the place value of the underlined digit.

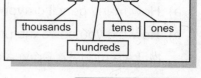

REMEMBER:

4 3 7 5

thousands   tens   ones   hundreds

   a) 35<u>6</u>4   `tens`   b) 1<u>3</u>36

   c) 25<u>6</u>   d) <u>1</u>230

   e) <u>3</u>859   f) 5<u>7</u>45   g) 2<u>3</u>8

2. Write the number for the following words.

   a) Three thousand four hundred twenty-five _____

   b) Four thousand eight hundred thirty-three _____

   c) Nine thousand six hundred seven _____

   d) Eight hundred six _____

3. Write the number words for the following numerals.

   a) 3 2 7 1 _____

   b) 5 8 9 3 _____

   c) 1 2 3 1 _____

4. Write each number in expanded form (using numerals).

   a) 3 0 7 5 = ____3000 + 70 + 5____   b) 3 2 7 5 = _____

   c) 9 7 0 1 = _____   d) 8 0 0 1 = _____

5. Circle the greater number.

   a) 2 7 3 8   OR   2 7 3 9

   b) 8 5 2 7   OR   Eight thousand five hundred thirty

BONUS

6. Add or subtract.

   a)   2 3 7 1
      + 5 2 8 3
      _____

   b)   1 3 8 0
      + 2 8 1 7
      _____

   c)   5 3 2 7
      − 4 1 1 4
      _____

   d)   9 3 2 1
      − 1 5 1 0
      _____

Answer the following questions in your notebook.

1. Tanya has 12 pencil crayons. Some are at school and 8 are at home.

   a) How many pencil crayons are at school?

   b) How did you solve the problem? (Did you use a calculation?
       Make a model? Draw a picture?)

---

2. Here are the heights of some of Canada's tallest towers.

   a) Write the heights in order from least to greatest.

   b) How much higher than the Calgary Tower is the
       Scotia Plaza?

   c) How much higher than the shortest tower is the
       tallest tower?

Heights of Buildings	
First Canadian Place, Toronto	298 m
Scotia Plaza, Toronto	275 m
Calgary Tower, Calgary	191 m

---

3. Place the numbers 1, 2, 3, 4 in the top four
   boxes to make the greatest possible sum and
   the greatest possible difference.

4. Find the error in Bob's sum.

$$
\begin{array}{r}
2 \\
4\,7 \\
+\,2\,5 \\
\hline
8\,1
\end{array}
$$

---

5. A baby whale drinks about 100 litres of milk
   each day.

   a) How many litres of milk will a baby whale
       drink in 7 days?

   b) What method of computation did you use
       to solve the problem?

   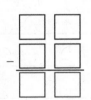

6. a) Write the number that is 10 greater
       than 200.

   b) Write the number that is 10 less
       than 200.

---

7. Pens cost 53¢.
   Erasers cost 44¢.
   Eric has 98¢.

   Does he have enough money
   to buy a pen and an eraser?

   Explain how you know.

8. Sam wants to add the numbers below.
   He starts by adding the ones digits.

$$
\begin{array}{r}
1 \\
2\,5 \\
+\,3\,7 \\
\hline
2
\end{array}
$$

   *Explain why Sam wrote
   the number 1 here.*

In the **array** below, there are 3 **rows** of dots. There are 5 dots **in each row**.

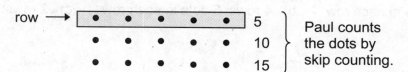

row → • • • • •   5 }
       • • • • •   10 } Paul counts
       • • • • •   15 } the dots by
                        skip counting.

He writes a multiplication statement for the array: **3 × 5 = 15**   (3 rows of 5 dots is 15 dots)

----

1. How many rows? How many dots in each row?

a)
• •
• •
• •

_____ rows

_____ dots in each row

b)
• • • •
• • • •
• • • •

_____ rows

_____ dots in each row

c)
• • • • • •
• • • • • •
• • • • • •

_____

_____

2. How many rows? How many dots in each row? Write a multiplication statement and find the answer by skip counting.

skip count:

a)
• • • •   **4**

• • • •   **8**

___2___ rows

___4___ dots in each row

___2 × 4 = 8_____

b)
• • • •
• • • •
• • • •

_____ rows

_____ dots in each row

_____

c)
• • • • •
• • • • •
• • • • •

_____

_____

_____

d)
• • •
• • •
• • •
• • •

_____ rows

_____ dots in each row

_____

e)
• • • •
• • • •
• • • •
• • • •

_____ rows

_____ dots in each row

_____

f)
• • •
• • •
• • •
• • •

_____

_____

_____

3. Draw an array and write a multiplication sentence for each question.

    a) 3 rows; 4 dots in each row   b) 4 rows; 5 dots in each row   c) 2 rows; 3 dots in each row

    _____   _____   _____

4. Write a multiplication statement for each array.

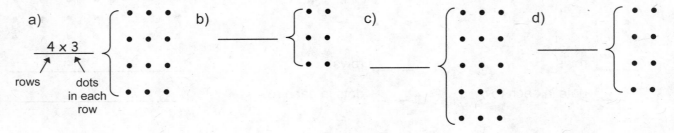

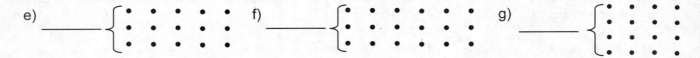

5. Draw arrays for these products.

    a) 3 × 5   b) 3 × 4   c) 4 × 6   d) 3 × 7   e) 1 × 5   f) 0 × 3

6. Use counters or draw arrays (of dots or squares) to model each question. Write a multiplication statement for each question.

    a) On a bus, 4 people can sit in a row.
        There are 5 rows of seats on the bus.
        How many people can ride on the bus?

    b) Peter puts 6 stamps in each row of his stamp book.
        There are 3 rows of stamps.
        How many stamps are there altogether?

    c) John plants 5 rows of trees with 3 trees in each row.
        How many trees did John plant?

7. Draw an array showing 2 × 3 and 3 × 2. Are the products 2 × 3 and 3 × 2 the same or different?
    How do you know?

1. Add the following numbers. (Keep a record of your sums in the boxes.)

Example   2 + 3 + 6 = ___ $\xrightarrow{\text{add } 2 + 3}$ (= 5)   ⬜5 2 + 3 + 6 = ___ $\xrightarrow{\text{add } 5 + 6}$ (= 11)   ⬜5 2 + 3 + 6 = 11

a) 3 + 4 + 1 = ___

b) 2 + 4 + 3 = ___

c) 1 + 3 + 2 = ___

d) 2 + 3 + 4 = ___

e) 3 + 2 + 3 = ___

f) 2 + 1 + 5 = ___

g) 3 + 2 + 1 + 4 = ___

h) 2 + 2 + 2 + 2 = ___

i) 5 + 5 + 5 + 5 = ___

2. Write an addition statement for each picture.
   Then add the numbers to find out how many apples there are altogether.

a) 3 boxes; 2 apples in each box

_____

b) 4 boxes; 3 apples in each box

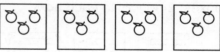

_____

c) 2 boxes; 4 apples in each box

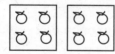

_____

d) 4 boxes; 5 apples in each box

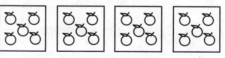

_____

3. Draw a picture and write an addition statement for your picture.

a) 4 boxes
   2 apples in each box

b) 3 boxes
   5 pencils in each box

c) 3 fish bowls
   4 fish in each bowl

d) 3 boats
   3 kids in each boat

4. Write an addition statement for each amount.

a) 4 boxes
   3 dimes in each box

b) 4 wagons
   2 kids in each wagon

c) 5 baskets
   6 oranges in each basket

NS3-36: Multiplication and Repeated Addition

Multiplication is a short way of writing the addition of the same number many times.

$$4 \times 3 = 3 + 3 + 3 + 3$$

add 3 four times

- -

1. Complete the number sentence using repeated addition.

   a) $4 \times 2 =$ _____

   b) $3 \times 2 =$ _____

   c) $3 \times 4 =$ _____

   d) $4 \times 5 =$ _____

   e) $2 \times 3 =$ _____

   f) $1 \times 5 =$ _____

2. Write a multiplication statement for each addition statement. The first one is done for you.

   a) $2 + 2 + 2 = 3 \times 2$

   b) $4 + 4 + 4 =$ _____

   c) $5 + 5 =$ _____

   d) $6 + 6 + 6 + 6 =$ _____

   e) $7 + 7 + 7 + 7 + 7 =$ _____

   f) $9 + 9 + 9 =$ _____

   g) $3 + 3 + 3 =$ _____

   h) $8 + 8 + 8 + 8 =$ _____

   i) $5 + 5 + 5 =$ _____

3. Circle the addition statements that cannot be written as multiplication statements.

   $2 + 2 + 2 \qquad 3 + 4 + 3 \qquad 2 + 5 + 7 \qquad 6 + 6 + 6 + 6 \qquad 8 + 8 + 9 + 8$

4. Write an addition statement and a multiplication statement.

   a) 3 boxes; 2 pencils in each box

   b) 4 boxes; 5 pencils in each box

   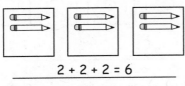

   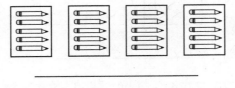

   $2 + 2 + 2 = 6$

   _____

   $3 \times 2 = 6$

   _____

   c) 2 boxes; 2 pencils in each box

   d) 4 boxes; 3 pencils in each box

   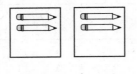

   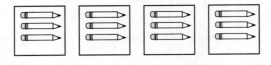

   _____

   _____

   _____

   _____

   e) 3 boxes
      5 pencils in each box

   f) 2 boats
      7 kids in each boat

   g) 4 pages
      5 stamps on each page

   _____

   _____

   _____

   _____

   _____

   _____

5. Change two numbers and then rewrite each addition statement as a multiplication statement.

   a) $2 + 2 + 3 + 1 = \mathbf{2 + 2 + 2 + 2} = \mathbf{4 \times 2} = \mathbf{8}$

   b) $3 + 2 + 3 + 4 + 3$

   c) $4 + 4 + 4 + 2 + 6$

Number Sense 1

NS3-37: Multiplying by Skip Counting

When you multiply a pair of numbers, the result is called the **product** of the numbers.

Lee finds the product of 3 and 4 by skip counting on a number line. He counts off three 4s:

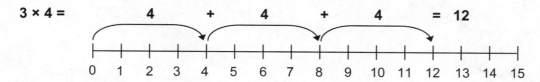

$$3 \times 4 = \quad 4 \quad + \quad 4 \quad + \quad 4 \quad = 12$$

From the picture, Lee can see that the product of 3 and 4 is **12**.

---

1. Show how to find the products by skip counting. Use arrows like the ones in Lee's picture above.

a) **3 x 2 =**

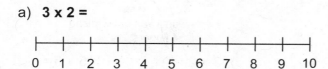

b) **4 x 2 =**

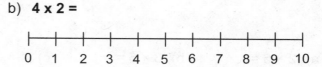

c) **2 x 3 =**

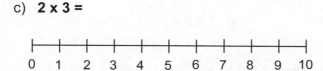

d) **2 x 5 =**

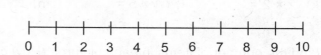

e) **1 x 5 =**

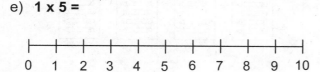

f) **4 x 1 =**

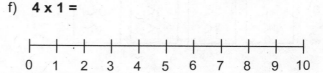

2. Use the number line to skip count by 2s, 3s, 4s and 5s. Fill in the boxes as you count.

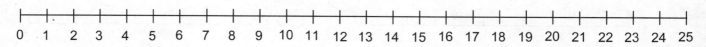

a)

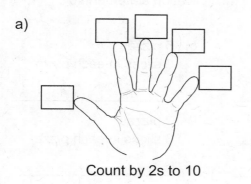

Count by 2s to 10

b)

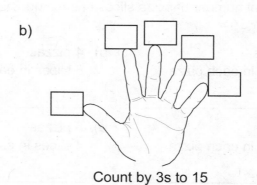

Count by 3s to 15

c)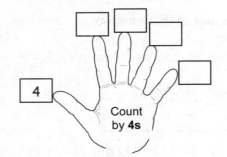

d)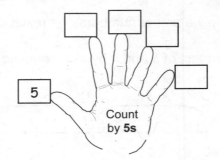

Count by **4s**

Count by **5s**

3. Find the products by skip counting on your fingers. Use the hands from Question 2 to help.

count by **5s**

 5   10   15   20

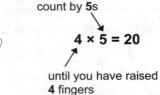

4 × 5 = 20

until you have raised **4 fingers**

a) 2 × 5 =

b) 3 × 5 =

c) 4 × 2 =

d) 3 × 2 =

e) 5 × 5 =

f) 2 × 3 =

g) 4 × 3 =

h) 2 × 4 =

i) 5 × 4 =

j) 4 × 4 =

k) 2 × 2 =

l) 1 × 5 =

m) 1 × 3 =

n) 3 × 3 =

o) 1 × 2 =

4. Find the number of items in each picture. (How can you use skip counting to help?) Write a multiplication statement for each picture.

a)

b)

_____

_____

c)

d)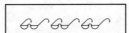

_____

_____

5. Find the total number of pizza slices in each question. Write a multiplication statement for your answer.

a) 3 pizzas
    4 slices in each pizza

b) 4 pizzas
    5 slices in each pizza

c) 5 pizzas
    3 slices in each pizza

_____

_____

_____

d) 2 pizzas
    5 slices in each pizza

e) 5 pizzas
    4 slices in each pizza

f) 3 pizzas
    3 slices in each pizza

_____

_____

_____

Amy knows how to find 3 × 6 by adding three 6s (6 + 6 + 6 = 18). Her teacher asks her how she can find 4 × 6 <u>quickly</u> (without adding four 6s).

Amy knows that 4 × 6 is one more 6 than 3 × 6. She shows this in two ways:

<u>With a picture</u>

four 6s {

three 6s

plus one more 6

<u>By adding</u>

$$4 × 6 = 6 + 6 + 6 + 6$$

four 6s   three 6s   plus one more 6

three 6s   plus one more 6

Amy knows that: **4 × 6 = 3 × 6 + 6**

So she finds 4 × 6 by adding 6 to 3 × 6 (= 18): 4 × 6 = **18** + 6 = **24**

----

1. Use each array to write a multiplication and addition statement. The first one is done for you.

a)   4 × 5   }   3 × 5

rows   dots in
each row

+   5

| 4 × 5 = 3 × 5 + 5 |

b)   {   ___

+   ___

c)   ___ {   ___

+   ___

d)   ___ {   ___

+   ___

e)   ___ {   ___

+   ___

f)   ___ {   ___

+   ___

2. In your notebook, draw an array (or use counters) to show that.

a) 3 × 6 = 2 × 6 + 6   b) 5 × 3 = 4 × 3 + 3   c) 3 × 8 = 2 × 8 + 8

3. You can always turn a product into a smaller product and a sum:

$$5 \times 3 = \mathbf{4} \times 3 + \mathbf{3} \qquad\qquad 9 \times 4 = \mathbf{8} \times 4 + \mathbf{4}$$

Take 1 away from 5.   *Add an extra 3.*   *Take 1 away from 9.*   *Add an extra 4.*

Turn each product into a smaller product and a sum.

a) $4 \times 2 = 3 \times$ __2__ $+$ _____

b) $5 \times 7 = 4 \times$ _____ $+$ _____

c) $8 \times 3 = 7 \times$ _____ $+$ _____

d) $3 \times 6 = 2 \times$ _____ $+$ _____

e) $7 \times 4 =$ _____ $\times$ _____ $+$ _____

f) $9 \times 6 =$ _____ $\times$ _____ $+$ _____

g) $5 \times 4 =$ _____

h) $8 \times 7 =$ _____

i) $7 \times 6 =$ _____

j) $6 \times 4 =$ _____

4. Find each answer by turning the product into a smaller product and a sum. The first one has been done for you.

a) $5 \times 3 = 4 \times 3 + 3$
   $= 12 + 3$
   $= 15$

b) $6 \times 3 =$
   $=$
   $=$

c) $6 \times 4 =$
   $=$
   $=$

d) $4 \times 4 =$
   $=$
   $=$

e) $6 \times 6 =$
   $=$
   $=$

f) $3 \times 7 =$
   $=$
   $=$

5. Solve. Be sure to show your work. The first one is done for you.

a) If $6 \times 5 = 30$,
   what is 7×5?

   $7 \times 5 = 6 \times 5 + 5$
      $= 30 + 5$
      $= 35$

b) If $8 \times 3 = 24$,
   what is 9×3?

c) If $7 \times 4 = 28$,
   what is 8×4?

d) If $10 \times 2 = 20$,
   what is 11×2?

NS3-39: Doubles

1. Count by 2s.

   2 , 4 , 6 , _____, _____, _____, _____, _____, _____

2. Double each number mentally by doubling the ones digit and the tens digit separately.

	24	14	12	32	64	22	13
Double	48						

	82	51	34	54	92	74	71
Double							

3. Double the ones and tens separately and add the result: 2 × 27 = 2 × 20 + 2 × 7 = 40 + 14 = 54.

	16	15	25	37	28	18	48
Double							

	17	45	66	35	46	29	55
Double							

4. Use doubles to find the missing products.

If 2 x 7 = 14	3 x 7 = 21	4 x 7 = 28	2 x 6 = 12
Then 4 x 7 =	6 x 7 =	8 x 7 =	4 x 6 =

3 x 6 = 18	4 x 6 = 24	2 x 8 = 16	4 x 8 = 32
6 x 6 =	8 x 6 =	4 x 8 =	8 x 8 =

2 x 9 = 18	3 x 9 = 27	4 x 9 = 36	2 x 12 = 24
4 x 9 =	6 x 9 =	8 x 9 =	4 x 12 =

5. Calculate the total cost of 2 items mentally.

   a) 2 oranges for 42¢ each _____

   b) 2 stickers for 37¢ each _____

   c) 2 stamps for 48¢ each _____

   d) 2 gold fish for 35¢ each _____

NS3-40: Topics in Multiplication

1. Use skip counting to find out how many legs the animals have.

Animals	Number of animals				
	1	**2**	**3**	**4**	**5**
🐌	0				
🐦	2				
🐈	4				
🐝	6				
🕷	8				

2. A hockey line has 5 players.
   Fill in the missing information.

_____ lines	5 + 5 + 5 + 5	4 × 5
3 lines	5 + 5 + 5	
6 lines		
_____ lines		2 × 5

3. Fill in the missing numbers.

   a) 4, 8, _____, 16, 20

   b) 5, _____, 15, _____, 25

   c) _____, 6, _____, 12, 15

   d) _____, _____, _____, 8, 10

4. Philip practices guitar twice a week. How many times will he practice in 4 weeks?

5. Carmen can ride 1 kilometre in 5 minutes. How far can she ride in 20 minutes?

6. Create a multiplication problem using the numbers 4 and 6.

7.
```
• • • •     • • •     • •     •
• • • •     • • •     • •     •
2 × 4 = 8   2 × 3 = 6   2 × 2 = 4   2 × 1 = 2   2 × 0 = 2
```

   Draw a similar set of arrays for 3 × 4, 3 × 3, 3 × 2, 3 × 1 and 3 × 0.

8. How many times as many circles are in box B as in box A?

HINT: Put the circles in box B into groups that contain as many circles as box A.

a)  _____three times as many circles_____

b)

_____

c)

_____

d)

_____

9. Draw …

a) 2 times as many triangles (or twice as many)

b) 3 times as many

c) 4 times as many

10. a) Kyle   Rema

b) Sam   Ravi

Rema has ____ times as many stickers as Kyle.   Ravi has ____ times as many stickers as Sam.

11. The magnifying glass makes each object look twice as big.

Actual length of object	Length under the magnifying glass
2 cm	
5 cm	
7 cm	

12. Kyle has 6 books. Ron has three times as many books.
Explain how you would find out how many books Ron has.

Answer these questions in your notebook.

1. A stool has 3 legs.
   How many legs will 6 stools have?

2. Terry multiplied 5 by a number less than 4.
   The ones digit of her answer was 0.
   What number did she multiply 5 by?
   And what was her answer?

3. Pens come in packages of 4.
   How many pens are in 4 packages?

4. Find two numbers (☐ and △) so that the multiplication statement ☐ × △ = ☐ is true.

5. What happens when you multiply a number by 1? What does 1 × 100 equal? What is 1 × 2 732?

6. Write all the pairs of numbers you can think of that multiply to give 12.

   (For an extra challenge, find all pairs of numbers that multiply to give 20.)

7. The **product** of 3 and 2 is 6 (3 × 2 = 6).

   The **sum** of 3 and 2 is 5 (3 + 2 = 5).

   Which is greater: the **sum** or the **product**?

8. Try finding the **sum** and the **product** of some other pairs of numbers.

   For instance, try 3 and 4, 2 and 5, 5 and 6, 1 and 7. What do you notice?

   Is the product always greater than the sum?

   Can they be the same?

9. This chart shows the multiplication facts for the numbers 1 to 6.

×	1	2	3	4	5	6
1	1	2	3			
2	2	4	6			
3	3	6	9			
4						
5						
6						

a) Fill in the missing numbers in the times table.

b) Describe any patterns you see in the rows of the times table.

c) Can you explain the patterns?

NS3-42: Pennies, Nickels and Dimes

1. Write the name and value of each coin.

 Name _____   Name _____   Name _____

Value _____   Value _____   Value _____

2. Answer the following questions. **HINT: Look at the pictures.**

a) How many pennies do you need to make a nickel? _____

b) How many pennies do you need to make a dime? _____

c) How many nickels do you need to make a dime? _____

3. Count by 5s starting from the given numbers:

a) 5, _____, _____, _____, _____   b) 35, _____, _____, _____, _____

c) 20, _____, _____, _____, _____   d) 60, _____, _____, _____, _____

e) 70, _____, _____, _____, _____   f) 90, _____, _____, _____, _____

4. Count on by 5s from the given number:

a) 15, _____, _____, _____, _____   b) 75, _____, _____, _____, _____

c) 40, _____, _____, _____, _____   d) 85, _____, _____, _____, _____

5. Count by 10s starting from the given numbers:

a) 20, _____, _____, _____, _____   b) 60, _____, _____, _____, _____

c) 45, _____, _____, _____, _____   d) 85, _____, _____, _____, _____

e) 15, _____, _____, _____, _____   f) 90, _____, _____, _____, _____

6. Count on by 10s from the given number:

a) 10, _____, _____, _____, _____   b) 35, _____, _____, _____, _____

jump math
MULTIPLYING POTENTIAL.

Number Sense 1

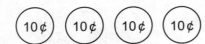

c) 70, _____, _____, _____, _____   d) 85, _____, _____, _____, _____

7. Count by the first number given, then by the second number after the vertical line.

a) __5__ , __10__ , __15__ | __16__ , __17__ , __18__ , __19__

        Count by 5s   *Continue counting by 1s*

b) __5__ , ___ | ___ , ___ , ___ , ___ , ___

        Count by 5s   *Continue counting by 1s*

c) __5__ , ___ , ___ , ___ , ___ | ___

        Count by 5s   *Continue counting by 1s*

d) __5__ , ___ , ___ , ___ | ___ , ___

        Count by 5s   *Continue counting by 1s*

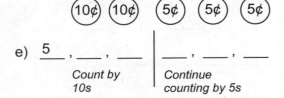

e) __5__ , ___ , ___ | ___ , ___ , ___

        Count by 10s   *Continue counting by 5s*

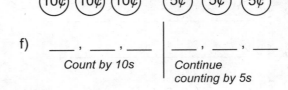

f) ___ , ___ , ___ | ___ , ___ , ___

        Count by 10s   *Continue counting by 5s*

8. Complete each pattern by counting by the first coin, then – after it switches – by the second coin.

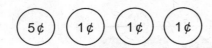

a) __5__ , __6__ , __7__ , __8__   b) ___ , ___ , ___ , ___

c) ___ , ___ , ___ , ___   d) ___ , ___ , ___ , ___ , ___

BONUS

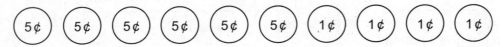

e) ___ , ___ , ___ , ___ , ___ , ___ , ___ , ___ , ___ , ___

1. Write the name and the value of the coin.

Name _____

Value _____

There are many ways of making a quarter with different combinations of coins:

See how many ways you can find using play money.

2. a) How many pennies make a quarter?

   _____

   b) How many nickels make a quarter?

   _____

   c) Can you make a quarter with dimes only?

   _____

3. Mick has two dimes. In order to equal a quarter ...

   a) how many nickels does he need? _____

   b) how many pennies does he need? _____

4. Circle the combinations of coins below that add up to a quarter.

a)

b)

c)

d)

e)

f)

5. Count by 25s: _____ , _____ , _____ , _____ , _____ , _____ , _____ , _____

NS3-44: Counting by Two or More Coin Values

1. Complete each pattern by counting by 25s, then by the number after the vertical line. The first one is done for you.

a) (25¢) (25¢) (25¢) (1¢) (1¢)

   _25_ , _50_ , _75_ | _76_ , _77_

   Count by 25s | *Count by 1s*

b) (25¢) (25¢) (25¢) (5¢) (5¢)

   ____ , ____ , ____ | ____ , ____

   Count by 25s | *Count by 5s*

c) (25¢) (25¢) (1¢) (1¢)

   ____ , ____ | ____ , ____

   Count by 25s | *Count by 1s*

d) (25¢) (25¢) (25¢) (10¢) (10¢)

   ____ , ____ , ____ | ____ , ____

   Count by 25s | *Count by 10s*

2. Complete each pattern by counting by the denominations given. The first one is done for you.

(25¢) (25¢) (10¢) (10¢)

a) _25_ , _50_ , _60_ , _70_

(25¢) (25¢) (25¢) (5¢) (1¢)

b) ____ , ____ , ____ , ____ , ____

(25¢) (25¢) (25¢) (25¢) (1¢)

c) ____ , ____ , ____ , ____ , ____

(25¢) (5¢) (5¢) (5¢) (5¢)

d) ____ , ____ , ____ , ____ , ____

3. Write the total amount of money in cents for the number of coins given in the charts below.
   HINT: Count by the first amount, then count on by the second amount.

a)
Quarters	Dimes
1	2

Total amount =

b)
Quarters	Dimes
1	3

Total amount =

c)
Quarters	Nickels
3	1

Total amount =

d)
Dimes	Nickels
6	7

Total amount =

e)
Quarters	Pennies
1	8

Total amount =

f)
Dimes	Nickels
4	3

Total amount =

BONUS

g)
Quarters	Nickels	Pennies
3	1	2

Total amount =

h)
Quarters	Dimes	Nickels
2	2	5

Total amount =

4. Complete each pattern by counting by the numbers given.

a)

  <u>10</u> , <u>20</u> , <u>30</u> | <u>35</u> , <u>40</u> | <u>41</u>

  Count by 10s | Count by 5s | Count by 1s

b)
  ____ , ____ | ____ , ____ | ____ , ____ , ____

  Count by 25s | Count by 10s | Count by 1s

c)
  ____ , ____ | ____ , ____ | ____ , ____

  Count by 25s | Count by 5s | Count by 1s

d)
  ____ , ____ , ____ | ____ , ____ , ____ | ____ , ____

  Count by 25s | Count by 10s | Count by 5s

BONUS

e)
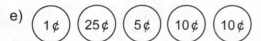

  ____ , ____ | ____ , ____ , ____ | ____ , ____ | ____ , ____

  Count by 25s | Count by 10s | Count by 5s | Count by 1s

5. Count the given coins and write the total amount.
   HINT: Count the bigger amounts first.

a) (1¢) (1¢) (5¢) (5¢) (10¢)

  Total amount =

b) (10¢) (25¢) (25¢) (1¢)

  Total amount =

c) (5¢) (25¢) (10¢) (10¢)

  Total amount =

d) (5¢) (10¢) (25¢) (5¢) (1¢) (1¢)

  Total amount =

e) (1¢) (25¢) (5¢) (10¢) (10¢)

  Total amount =

f) (25¢) (10¢) (1¢) (1¢) (10¢)

  Total amount =

g) (1¢) (1¢) (5¢) (25¢) (5¢) (1¢) (10¢) (10¢) (25¢)

  Total amount =

BONUS

6. Complete each pattern by counting on by each denomination.

(25¢) (25¢) (25¢) (25¢) (10¢) (10¢) (5¢) (5¢) (1¢)

  ____ , ____ , ____ , ____ , ____ , ____ , ____ , ____ , ____

TEACHER: Allow your students to practise the skill in Question 5 with play money.

NS3-45: Counting by Different Denominations

1. Fill in the missing amounts, counting by 5s.

| a) 12, ____ , 22 | b) 30, ____ , ____ , 45 | c) 67, ____ , ____ , 82 |
| d) 18, ____ , ____ , 33 | e) 81, ____ , ____ , 96 | f) 45, ____ , ____ , 60 |

2. Fill in the missing amounts, counting by 10s.

| a) 6, ____ , 26 | b) 21, ____ , ____ , 51 | c) 49, ____ , ____ , 79 |

3. Write in the missing coin to complete the addition statement. The possibilities for each question are listed.

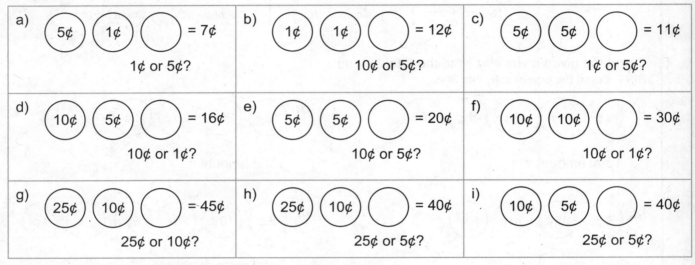

4. Draw the additional **pennies** needed to make the total.

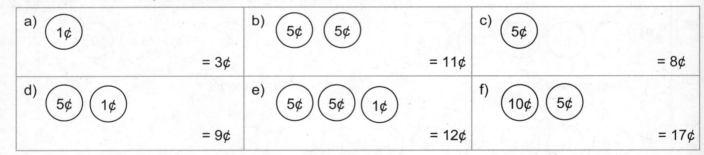

5. Draw the additional **nickels** needed to make the total.

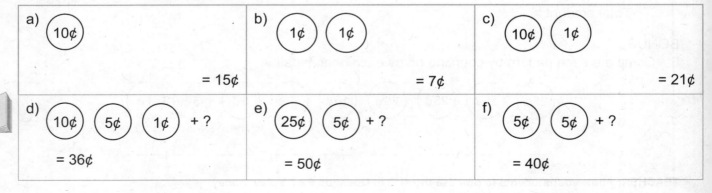

6. Draw the additional **dimes** needed to make the total.

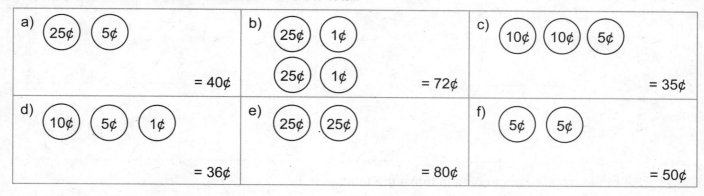

| a) 25¢ 5¢ = 40¢ | b) 25¢ 1¢ / 25¢ 1¢ = 72¢ | c) 10¢ 10¢ 5¢ = 35¢ |
| d) 10¢ 5¢ 1¢ = 36¢ | e) 25¢ 25¢ = 80¢ | f) 5¢ 5¢ = 50¢ |

7. Draw the additional **coins** needed to make each total.

a) 25¢ + _How many nickels?_ = 35¢	b) 10¢ + _How many dimes?_ = 50¢
c) 25¢ 25¢ + _How many dimes?_ = 70¢	d) 25¢ 5¢ + _How many nickels?_ = 35¢
e) 10¢ 10¢ + _How many nickels?_ = 35¢	f) 25¢ 25¢ + _How many quarters?_ = 75¢

BONUS

8. Draw the additional coins needed to make each total. You can only use **two** coins for each question, either (i) a penny and a nickel, (ii) a penny and a dime, or (iii) a nickel and a dime.

a) 16¢ 10¢	b) 17¢ 10¢ 1¢
c) 30¢ 10¢ 5¢	d) 50¢ 25¢ 10¢
e) 26¢ 10¢ 1¢	f) 61¢ 25¢ 25¢

9. Draw a picture to show the **extra coins** each child will need to pay for the item they want:

   a) Kevin has 25¢. He wants to buy a pen for 35¢.

   b) Sandra has 1 quarter and 2 dimes. She wants to buy a notebook for 70¢.

   c) Laura has 2 quarters, 1 dime and 1 nickel. She wants to buy a snack for 87¢.

10. Can you make 27¢ using only nickels and dimes? Explain why or why not.

 jump math
MULTIPLYING POTENTIAL.

NS3-46: Least Number of Coins

1. Use the *least* number of coins to make the totals. Draw in the coins.

a) 6¢	b) 4¢
c) 8¢	d) 9¢

2. Use the *least* number of coins to make the totals.
   HINT: Start by seeing how many dimes you need.

a) 12¢ (10¢)(1¢)(1¢) *correct* (5¢)(5¢)(1¢)(1¢) *incorrect*	b) 14¢
c) 21¢	d) 23¢

3. Use the *least* number of coins to make the totals.

a) 15¢	b) 20¢

4. Use the *least* number of coins.
   HINT: Start by seeing how many dimes you need (if any), then nickels and then pennies.

a) 16¢	b) 22¢
c) 11¢	d) 8¢
e) 24¢	f) 17¢
g) 14¢	h) 19¢

5. Fill in the amounts: 2 quarters = _____ ¢   3 quarters = _____ ¢   4 quarters = _____ ¢

6. Ron has 85¢ in coins in his pocket. What is the greatest number of coins that could be quarters?

NS3-46: Least Number of Coins (continued)

7. For each amount, what is the greatest amount you could pay in quarters?

Amount	Greatest amount you could pay in quarters	Amount	Greatest amount you could pay in quarters
a) 35¢		b) 78¢	
c) 52¢		d) 62¢	
e) 31¢		f) 83¢	
g) 59¢		h) 27¢	

8. For each amount, find the greatest amount you could pay in quarters. Represent the amount remaining using the least number of coins.

Amount	Amount Paid in Quarters	Amount Remaining	Amount Remaining in Coins
a) 81¢	75¢	81¢ – 75¢ = 6¢	(5¢) (1¢)
b) 57¢			
c) 31¢			
d) 85¢			

9. Use the **least** number of coins to make the totals.

a) 30¢	(10¢) (10¢) (10¢) (25¢) (5¢) *incorrect* *correct*	b) 76¢
c) 35¢		d) 50¢

10. Trade coins to make each amount with fewer coins. Draw a picture to show your answer.

a) (10¢) (5¢) (5¢)	b) (25¢) (5¢) (5¢) (5¢)	c) (10¢) (10¢) (5¢) (5¢)
d) (5¢) (5¢) (5¢) (5¢)	e) (5¢) (1¢) (1¢) (1¢) (1¢) (1¢)	f) (10¢) (10¢) (5¢) (5¢) (5¢)

11. How could you trade 3 dimes for fewer coins?

12. Show how you could make 42¢ using the least number of coins. Use play money to help you.

NS3-47: Dimes and Pennies

1. Write the number of dimes and pennies in each collection of coins. Then total each collection.

    a)   (10¢) (1¢) (1¢)

    ____ dimes + ____ pennies

    Total amount = _____

    b)   (10¢) (10¢) (1¢) (1¢)

    ____ dimes + ____ pennies

    Total amount = _____

    c)   (10¢) (1¢) (1¢) (1¢) (1¢)

    ____ dimes + ____ pennies

    Total amount = _____

    d)   (10¢) (10¢) (10¢) (10¢)

    ____ dimes + ____ pennies

    Total amount = _____

2. Give the total amount of money for the number of dimes and pennies in the T-tables below.

    a)
dimes	pennies
2	3

    = _____ ¢

    b)
dimes	pennies
7	0

    = _____ ¢

    c)
dimes	pennies
4	1

    = _____ ¢

    d)
dimes	pennies
8	2

    = _____ ¢

    e)
dimes	pennies
3	9

    = _____ ¢

    f)
dimes	pennies
1	8

    = _____ ¢

3. For each amount, write the number of dimes and pennies needed in each column of the tables.

    a)
dimes	pennies

    = 25¢

    b)
dimes	pennies

    = 40¢

    c)
dimes	pennies

    = 36¢

    d)
dimes	pennies

    = 2¢

    e)
dimes	pennies

    = 12¢

    f)
dimes	pennies

    = 99¢

BONUS

4. Draw the number of dimes and pennies you would need to make each amount.
    Then write the money amount in words.

    a) 30¢   b) 24¢   c) 51¢   d) 45¢   e) 33¢   f) 67¢

NS3-48: Making Change Using Mental Math

1. Calculate the change owing for each purchase.

   a) Price of a pen = 48¢
      Amount paid = 50¢

      Change = _____

   b) Price of a pencil = 47¢
      Amount paid = 50¢

      Change = _____

   c) Price of an eraser = 84¢
      Amount paid = 90¢

      Change = _____

   d) Price of a sticker = 52¢
      Amount paid = 60¢

      Change = _____

   e) Price of a marker = 74¢
      Amount paid = 80¢

      Change = _____

   f) Price of a notebook = 66¢
      Amount paid = 70¢

      Change = _____

 2. Find the change owing from a dollar (100¢).

Price	Change	Price	Change	Price	Change
a) 80¢		d) 40¢		g) 50¢	
b) 70¢		e) 60¢		h) 10¢	
c) 20¢		f) 30¢		i) 90¢	

3. Find the change owing for each purchase.

   a) Price of a pen = 50¢
      Amount Paid = $1.00

      Change = _____

   b) Price of an eraser = 80¢
      Amount paid = $1.00

      Change = _____

   c) Price of an apple = 20¢
      Amount paid = $1.00

      Change = _____

   d) Price of a banana = 60¢
      Amount paid = $1.00

      Change = _____

   e) Price of a patty = 90¢
      Amount paid = $1.00

      Change = _____

   f) Price of a pencil = 30¢
      Amount paid = $1.00

      Change = _____

   g) Price of a gumball = 10¢
      Amount paid = $1.00

      Change = _____

   h) Price of a juice = 40¢
      Amount paid = $1.00

      Change = _____

   i) Price of a popsicle = 70¢
      Amount paid = $1.00

      Change = _____

4. Find the smallest number ending in zero (i.e. 10, 20, 30, 40...) that is <u>greater</u> than the number given.

   a) 72 [80]   b) 63 [   ]   c) 49 [   ]   d) 27 [   ]   e) 55 [   ]   f) 6 [   ]

NS3-48: Making Change Using Mental Math *(continued)*

5. Make change for the amount written below. Follow the steps shown for 17¢.

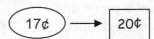

Step 1: *Find the smallest multiple of 10 greater than 17¢.*

Step 2: *Find the differences:* 20 – 17 and 100 – 20

Step 3: *Add the differences:* 3¢ + 80¢   **Change = 83¢**

a)

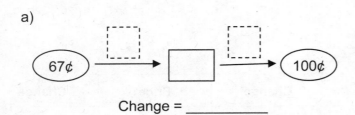

Change = _____

b)

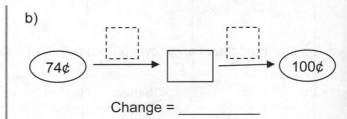

Change = _____

c)

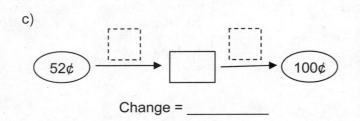

Change = _____

d)

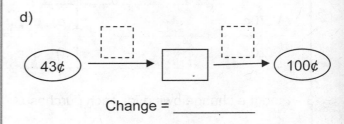

Change = _____

e)

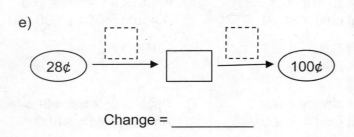

Change = _____

f)

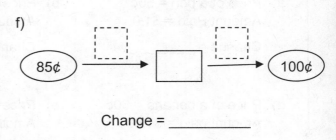

Change = _____

6. Find change from 100¢ for the following. Try to do the work in your head.

a) 88¢ _____   b) 65¢ _____   c) 26¢ _____   d) 47¢ _____   e) 55¢ _____

f) 37¢ _____   g) 95¢ _____   h) 58¢ _____   i) 87¢ _____   j) 92¢ _____

BONUS

7. Find the change for the following amount in your head.

a) Price: 36¢   Amount Paid: 50¢

Change Required: _____

b) Price: 56¢   Amount Paid: 75¢

Change Required: _____

TEACHER:
Review the meaning of the terms: "less than", "greater than", "odd", "even", "multiples of 2", "multiples of 3".

REMEMBER:
Zero is an even number and is also a multiple of any number.

1. Write the numbers from 0 to 9 in order.

2. Write all the numbers from 0 to 9 that are.

a) greater than 7

b) greater than 6

c) greater than 5

d) less than 4

e) less than 5

f) less than 2

g) greater than 8

h) less than 8

i) greater than 4

j) odd numbers

k) even numbers

l) multiples of 2

m) multiples of 3

n) multiples of 4

o) multiples of 5

3. Make two lists (and circle the numbers that appear on both lists) to find the numbers from 0 to 9 that are:

a) **odd numbers greater than 5**

   i) odd numbers: 1, 3, 5, (7), (9)

   ii) numbers greater than 5: 6, (7), 8, (9)

   Answer: 7, 9

b) **even numbers greater than 5**

   i) even numbers:

   ii) numbers greater than 5:

   Answer:

Number Sense 1

c) **odd numbers less than 3**

   i) odd numbers:

   ii) numbers less than 3:

   Answer:

d) **even numbers less than 6**

   i) even numbers:

   ii) numbers less than 6:

   Answer:

e) **odd numbers less than 5**

   i) odd numbers:

   ii) numbers less than 5:

   Answer:

f) **even numbers greater than 5**

   i) even numbers:

   ii) numbers greater than 5:

   Answer:

g) **numbers greater than 4 and less than 7**

   i) numbers greater than 4:

   ii) numbers less than 7:

   Answer:

h) **numbers greater than 3 and less than 5**

   i) numbers greater than 3:

   ii) numbers less than 5:

   Answer:

i) **even numbers that are multiples of 3**

   i) even numbers:

   ii) multiples of 3:

   Answer:

j) **odd numbers that are multiples of 3**

   i) odd numbers:

   ii) multiples of 3:

   Answer:

4. Write the numbers from 0 to 9 in order:

Then …

a) Circle the number that is greater than 8.

b) Underline the number that is less than 1.

c) Cross out the number that is less than 8 and greater than 6.

Many problems in mathematics and science have more than one solution.

If a problem involves two quantities, you can be sure you haven't missed any possible solutions if you list the values of one of the quantities in increasing order.

For instance, to find all the ways you can make 35¢ with dimes and nickels, start by assuming you have no dimes, then 1 dime, and so on up to 3 dimes (4 would be too many).

In each case, count on by 5s to 35 to find out how many nickels you need to make 35¢:

Step 1:

dimes	nickels
0	
1	
2	
3	

Step 2:

dimes	nickels
0	7
1	5
2	3
3	1

---

1. Fill in the amount of pennies or nickels you need to ...

a) ... make 15¢

dimes	nickels
0	
1	

b) ... make 25¢

dimes	nickels
0	
1	
2	

c) ... make 12¢

nickels	pennies
0	
1	
2	

d) ... make 18¢

nickels	pennies
0	
1	
2	
3	

e) ... make 65¢

quarters	nickels
0	
1	
2	

f) ... make 85¢

quarters	nickels
0	
1	
2	
3	

2.

dimes	nickels
0	
1	
2	

Sharon wants to find all the ways she can make 25¢ using dimes and nickels. Why did she stop at 2 dimes?

_____

_____

3. Fill in the amount of pennies, nickels, dimes, or quarters you need to make …
   HINT: You may not need to use all of the rows.

a) 13¢

dimes	pennies

b) 35¢

dimes	nickels

c) 80¢

quarters	nickels

TEACHER:
Give your students practice with questions like the ones above before you allow them to continue.

4. Birds have 2 legs, cats have 4 legs, and ants have 6 legs. Complete the charts to find out how many legs each combination of 2 animals has.

a)

birds	cats	total number of legs
0	2	
1	1	
2	0	

b)

birds	ants	total number of legs
0	2	
1	1	
2	0	

5. Fill in the charts to find the solution to each problem.

a)

birds	dogs	total number of legs

2 pets have a total of 6 legs.
Each pet is either a bird or a dog.
How many birds and dogs?

b)

birds	cats	total number of legs

3 pets have a total of 8 legs.
Each pet is either a bird or cat.
How many birds and cats?

ME3-1: Estimating Lengths in Centimetres

1. A **centimetre** (cm) is a unit of measurement for **length** (or **height** or **thickness**).

    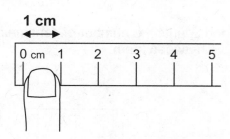

    Your index finger is approximately one centimetre wide.

    Measure the following objects using your index finger (or the finger closest to 1 cm):

    a) My pencil is approximately _____ cm long.   b) My JUMP book is about _____ cm wide.

2. Pick another object in the classroom to measure with your index finger:

    _____ is approximately _____ cm.

3. **2 cm** A penny is about 2 cm wide.

    How many pennies would you need to line up to make ...
    HINT: Skip count by 2s.

    a) 10 cm? _____   b) 20 cm? _____   c) 30 cm? _____

4. Hold up your hand to a ruler.

    How far do you have to spread your fingers to make your hand 10 cm wide?

    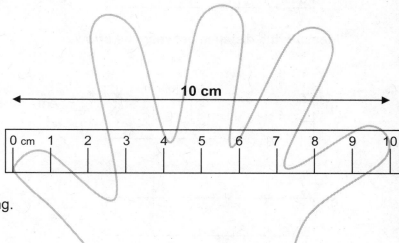

    Now measure the following objects in your classroom using your (measured) spread out hand:

    a) My workbook is approx. _____ cm long.

    b) My desk is approx. _____ cm wide.

    c) My arm is approx. _____ cm long.

    d) My leg is approx. _____ cm long.

5. Pick another object in the classrooms to measure with your hand:

    The _____ is approximately _____ cm long.

Midori counts the number of centimetres between the arrows by counting the number of "hops" it takes to move between them:

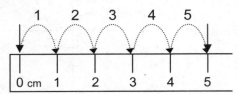

_5_ cm

---

1. Measure the distance between the two arrows by counting the number of centimetres between them.

a) 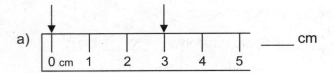 ____ cm   b) 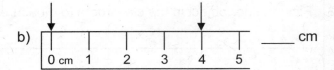 ____ cm

2. Measure the distance between the arrows.
   Count carefully – the first arrow is not at the beginning of the ruler.

a) 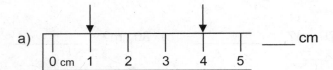 ____ cm   b)  ____ cm

3. Measure the distance between the arrows.

a) 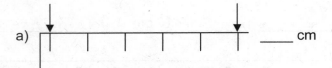 ____ cm   b) 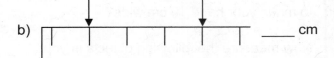 ____ cm

c) 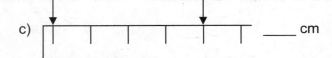 ____ cm   d)  ____ cm

e) 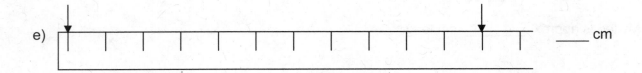 ____ cm

f) 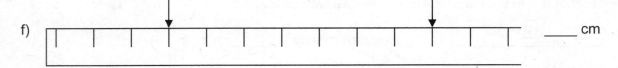 ____ cm

Laura measures the line by lining up her ruler with the endpoint of the line.

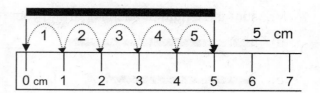

She counts the number of centimetre "hops" it takes to reach to the end of the line.

1. Measure the length of each line or object.

a) 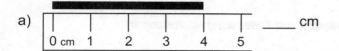 _____ cm

b) 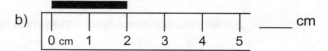 _____ cm

c) 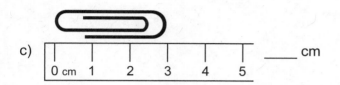 _____ cm

d) 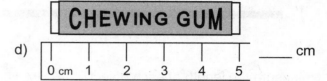 _____ cm

2. Measure the length of the lines and objects below.
   BE CAREFUL: The centimetre marks on these rulers are not numbered.

a)  _____ cm

b)  _____ cm

c) 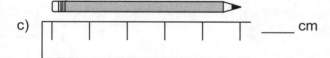 _____ cm

d) 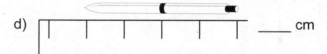 _____ cm

e) 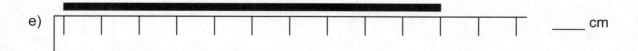 _____ cm

f) 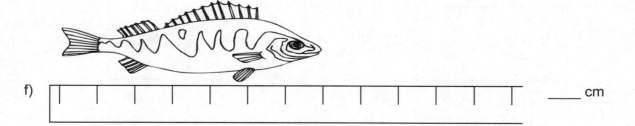 _____ cm

1. Measure the length of each line using your ruler.

a)  _____ cm   b) _____ cm

c)  _____ cm   d) _____ cm

e) _____ cm

f) _____ cm

g) _____ cm

h) _____ cm

i) _____ cm

2. Measure the length of each object.

a)  _____ cm   b)  CHEWING GUM _____ cm

c)  _____ cm   d) 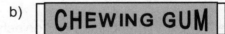 _____ cm

3. Measure the distance between the two points using your ruler.

a)   _____ cm   b)   _____ cm

c) _____ cm   d) _____ cm

BONUS

4. Measure all the sides of each shape.

a) _____ cm
   _____ cm   _____ cm
   _____ cm

b) _____ cm   _____ cm
   _____ cm

5. Measure the length of several objects on your desk (rulers, pencils, erasers, etc.)

ME3-5: Drawing to Centimetre Measurements

Blake is drawing a line 5 cm long.

He starts by drawing an arrow at the beginning of the ruler then counting in 5 centimetres:

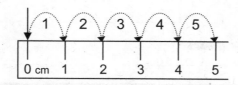

He draws a second arrow on the last centimetre mark that was counted to and then draws a line to connect the two arrows:

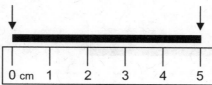

---

1. Draw two arrows on each ruler that are the given distance apart.
   HINT: You may find this easier if you place one of your arrows at the '0' mark.

   a) Two arrows 3 cm apart.   b) Two arrows 1 cm apart.   c) Two arrows 4 cm apart.

   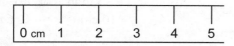 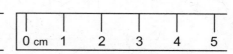

2. Use a ruler or straight edge to draw a line starting from the '0' mark of the ruler and ending at the given length.

   a) Draw a line 1 cm long.   b) Draw a line 4 cm long.   c) Draw a line 5 cm long.

   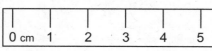 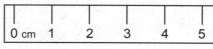 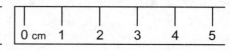

3. Draw a line ...

   a) 3 cm long   b) 7 cm long   c) 10 cm long

4. Draw each object to the exact measurement given:

   a) A caterpillar, 4 cm long.   b) A leaf, 9 cm long.   c) A spoon, 9 cm long.

BONUS
5. On grid paper, draw a rectangle with a width of 4 cm and a length of 5 cm.

Measurement 1

ME3-6: Estimating in Centimetres

1. Estimate whether each line is <u>less than</u> or <u>more than</u> 10 cm long. Place a checkmark in the appropriate column.

		LESS than 10 cm	MORE than 10 cm
a)	▬▬▬▬▬▬▬		
b)	▬▬▬▬▬▬▬▬▬▬		
c)	▬		
d)	▬▬▬▬▬▬▬		

2. How good were your estimates? Measure the length of each line in Question 1.

   a) _____ cm   b) _____ cm   c) _____ cm   d) _____ cm

3. Estimate whether the distance between the points is <u>less</u> than 10 cm or <u>more</u> than 10 cm.

		LESS than 10 cm	MORE than 10 cm
a)	● ●		
b)	● ●		
c)	● ●		
d)	● ●		

4. How good were your estimates? Measure the distance between the pairs of dots in Question 3.

   a) _____ cm   b) _____ cm   c) _____ cm   d) _____ cm

BONUS
5. Estimate the **length** of the boxes below to the nearest cm. Then check your estimate.

   a) [   ]   b) [   ]

   Estimate: _____ cm   Actual: _____ cm   Estimate: _____ cm   Actual: _____ cm

A **metre** is a unit of measurement for **length** (or **height** or **thickness**) equal to 100 cm.

A metre stick is 100 cm long:

- -

1. Ten interlocking centimetre
   cubes are 10 cm long.

   How many groups of ten cubes would make a metre?

You can estimate metres using parts of your body:

- A giant step is about a metre long.

- If you stretch your arms out the distance between
  the tips of your fingers is about one metre.
  (This distance is called your *arm span*.)

2. Take a giant step and ask a friend to measure your step with a piece of string.

   Hold the string up to a metre stick. Is your step more or less than a metre?

   _____

3. Ask a friend to measure your arm span using a piece of string.

   Is your arm span more or less than a metre?

   _____

4. Stand against a wall and ask a friend to measure your height with chalk and a metre stick:

   Your height is _____ cm.   Are you taller than 1 metre? _____

5. Estimate each distance to the nearest metre. Then measure the distance:

   a) The length of the blackboard in your classroom: Estimate - _____ m   Actual - _____ m

   b) The length of your desk: Estimate - _____ m   Actual - _____ m

   c) The distance from the floor to the door handle: Estimate - _____ m   Actual - _____ m

6. Find (or think of) an object in your classroom or outside that is approximately 2 metres long.

   _____

Here are some measurements you can use for estimating in metres:

about 2 metres	*about 2 metres*	*about 10 metres*	*about 100 metres*
			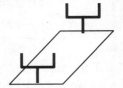
The height of a (tall) adult	The length of an adult's bicycle	The length of a school bus	The length of a football field

1. Five bikes (end to end) can park along a school wall. About how long is the wall?
    Use the estimates given above.

2. a) How many adults do you think could lie head to foot across your classroom?

    b) Approximately how wide is your classroom?

3. a) A typical floor in a building is about 4 m high. About how high is your school?

    b) If a school bus was tipped up on its end, would it be as high as your school?

    c) A car is about 3 metres long. How many cars high is your school?

4. a) About how many school buses can park along your school playground?

    b) How many metres long do you think your school playground is? Explain.

5. Count by 25s: 25, _____, _____, _____, _____, _____, _____, _____

6. An Olympic swimming pool
    is 25 metres **wide**:

    25 metres

    a) If you swim 3 widths, how many metres will you swim in total?

    b) If you swim 5 widths, how many metres will you swim?

7. Count by 50s: 50, _____, _____, _____, _____, _____, _____, _____, _____, _____

8. An Olympic swimming pool
    is 50 metres **long**:

    50 metres

    a) If you swim 3 lengths, how many metres will you swim in total?

    b) If you swim 4 lengths, how many metres will you swim?

    c) How many lengths would you need to swim to travel 100 metres?

    d) How many lengths would you need to swim to travel 500 metres?

9. A small city block is about 100 m long.
    Write the name of a place you can walk to from your school (a store, a park, your house).
    Approximately how many metres away from the school is the place you named?

ME3-9: Kilometres

A **kilometre** (km) is a unit of measurement for **length** equal to 1000 metres.

1. a) Skip count by 100s to find out how many times you need to add 100 to make 1000.

   _____

   b) A football field is about 100 m long. How many football fields long is a kilometre?

   _____

2. Count by 10s to find the number of times you need to add 10 to make each number.

   a) 100 = _____ tens

   b) 200 = _____ tens

   c) 300 = _____ tens

   d) 400 = _____ tens

   e) 500 = _____ tens

   f) 600 = _____ tens

3. Using the pattern in Question 3, how many times would you need to add 10 to make 1000?

4. A school bus is about 10 m long. How many school buses, line up end to end, would be ...

   a) close to a kilometre?

   b) close to 2 km?

   _____

   _____

5. Continue the pattern to find out how many times you need to add 2 to make 1000.

   a) 100 = __50__ twos

   b) 200 = __100__ twos

   c) 300 = __150__ twos

   d) 400 = __200__ twos

   e) 500 = _____ twos

   f) 600 = _____ twos

   g) 700 = _____ twos

   h) 800 = _____ twos

   i) 900 = _____ twos

   j) 1000 = _____ twos

6. A bike is about 2 m long.
   How many bikes, lined up, would make a kilometre?

   _____

7. If you lined up the following objects would they be:

   • close to 1 km,   • less than 1 km, or   • more than 1 km?

   Explain your answer.
   HINT: First decide if the individual object is close to a metre, less than a metre or more than a metre.

   a) 1000 paper clips   b) 1000 bikes   c) 1000 JUMP books   d) 1000 baseball bats

James uses a map to plan a trip to Nova Scotia and New Brunswick.
The numbers on the map are the lengths of the roads between the cities (in kilometres).

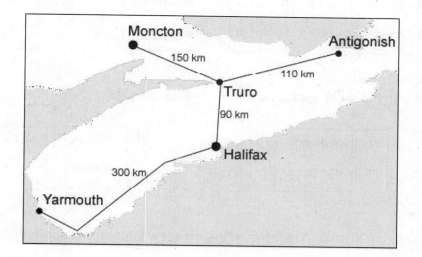

8. Fill in the blanks.

    a) Moncton and Truro are _____ km apart.

    b) Yarmouth and Halifax are _____ km apart.

    c) Truro and Antigonish are _____ km apart.

    d) Halifax and Truro are _____ km apart.

9. How far would you travel if you made the following trips?

    a) Start in Moncton. Drive through Truro to Antigonish – you would travel _____ km.

    b) Start in Yarmouth. Drive through Halifax to Truro – you would travel _____ km.

    c) Start in Halifax. Drive through Truro to Antigonish – you would travel _____ km.

    d) Start in Antigonish. Drive through Truro and Halifax to Yarmouth – you would travel _____ km.

BONUS
10. Look at the kilometre scale on a map of Canada.
    Estimate the distance between two cities.
    Explain how you made your estimate.
    Ask your teacher to check the actual distance in kilometres.

1. Match the word with the symbol.

a)
| cm | metre |
| m | centimetre |

b)
| cm | centimetre |
| km | kilometre |

c)
| km | kilometre |
| m | metre |

2. Match the object with the most appropriate unit of measurement.

a)
| metre | length of an ant |
| centimetre | height of a door |

b)
| metre | height of an adult |
| kilometre | distance to the moon |

3. Match the word with the symbol. Then match the object with the most appropriate unit of measurement.

a)
cm	kilometre	thickness of a book
m	centimetre	distance across an ocean
km	metre	height of the classroom

b)
km	metre	height of a door
cm	kilometre	distance to Rome
m	centimetre	length of a pencil

4. Order the following objects from shortest (1), to next shortest (2), to longest (3).

a) _____ Length of an ant

_____ Distance an airplane flies

_____ Height of an adult

b) _____ Length of a carrot

_____ Length of a bus

_____ Distance from Toronto, ON
to Victoria, BC

5. Order the following items from shortest to longest (1 = shortest, 2 = next shortest, 3 = longest). What unit would you use to measure each?

| cm | m | km |

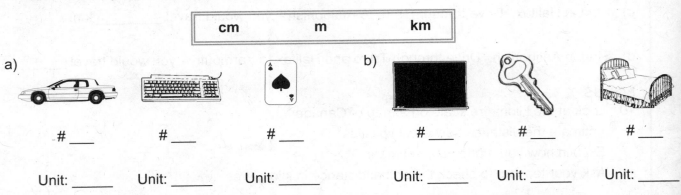

a)

\# ___   \# ___   \# ___

b)

\# ___   \# ___   \# ___

Unit: _____   Unit: _____   Unit: _____   Unit: _____   Unit: _____   Unit: _____

6. How many centimetres are in a metre? _____

7. Change the following measurements into centimetres.

   a) 3 m = _____ cm   b) 5 m = _____ cm   c) _____ cm = 2 m

8. Circle the larger amount.
   HINT: Change the measurement in metres (m) to centimetres (cm). Show your work in the box provided.

   a) 3 m   or   5 cm   b) 5 m   or   45 cm   c) 780 cm   or   6 m

   | cm | | cm | | cm |

9. Mark the measurements on the number line. (First change all measurements to cm.)

   A. 50 cm
   B. 1 m
   C. 2 m

   ```
   |-------|-------|-------|-------|
   0 cm   50 cm  100 cm  150 cm  200 cm
   ```

10. This chart shows the lengths of some snakes at the zoo.

Snake	Length
Garter Snake - **G**	150 cm
Coral Snake - **C**	50 cm
Fox Snake - **F**	100 cm
Boa Snake - **B**	2 m

Mark the lengths of **G**, **C**, **F** and **B** on the number line.

```
|------------------|------------------|
0 cm             100 cm            200 cm
```

11. Order the animals from lowest flier (1) to highest flier (5).

Animal	Greatest Height of Flight
Bat	50 m
Eagle	5 000 m
Blue Jay	2 000 m
Butterfly	25 m
Small insect	150 m

1. _____
2. _____
3. _____
4. _____
5. _____

12. Julie measured some lengths but forgot to record the unit of measurement. Fill in the correct units.

a) bed: 180 _____   b) bus: 10 _____   c) toothbrush: 16 _____   d) driveway: 10 _____

TEACHER:
Read these questions out loud to your students before you assign them.

13. Some BIG and SMALL facts about Canada!

Fill in the blanks with the correct unit: **cm**, **m**, or **km**.

a) Niagara Falls is 48 _____ high.

b) A racoon can grow to be 80 _____ long.

c) The St. Lawrence River is 3058 _____ long.

d) A black bear is 2 _____ long.

e) The width of a maple leaf is approximately 16 _____.

f) The Mackenzie River in the Northwest Territories is 4241 _____ long.

14. A horse can run 50 kilometres in an hour.

a) How far can you run in an hour?

b) Name a city or town about 50 kilometres from where you live.

15. What would you use to measure the following distances – metres or kilometres?
Explain one of your answers.
HINT: You can walk a kilometre in about 15 minutes (taking about 2000 steps).

a) From your class to the cafeteria.

b) From your home to school.

c) Between Toronto and Ottawa.

d) Around the school yard.

Rona wants to make a border for her picture using triangles:

She measures the top and right hand sides of her picture by placing triangles along the sides.

Virginia Falls (North West Territories)

To find the number of triangles she will need for her frame, Rona writes an addition statement.

4	+	3	+	4	+	3	=	**14** triangles
top side		right side		bottom side		left side		

The **perimeter** (or the distance around the outside) of Rona's picture measured in sides of triangles is 14 sides.

- -

1. Measure the following lines using pattern block triangles.
   (If you don't have pattern blocks, trace and cut out the triangle at the top of this page).

   a) _____   _____ triangles

   b) _____   _____ triangles

   c) _____   _____ triangles

2. Add the following numbers.
   HINT: Try grouping the first two numbers; then doubling. Why does this work?

   a) 3 + 1 + 3 + 1 = _____   b) 3 + 2 + 3 + 2 = _____   c) 5 + 2 + 5 + 2 = _____

   d) 4 + 3 + 4 + 3 = _____   e) 2 + 7 + 2 + 7 = _____   f) 6 + 4 + 6 + 4 = _____

   g) 10 + 6 + 10 + 6 = _____   h) 9 + 2 + 9 + 2 = _____   i) 11 + 3 + 11 + 3 = _____

3. Rona wants to put triangles along every side of a picture.
   Write an addition statement to find out how many triangles she will need altogether.

a)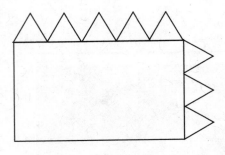

b)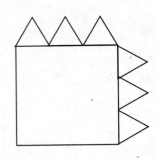

c)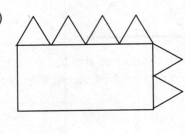

_____

4. Measure the perimeter of the figures using pattern block triangles.
   (You will only need one triangle – you can use it to mark of the proper lengths.)

a)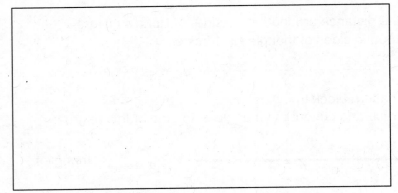

Perimeter = _____ triangles

b)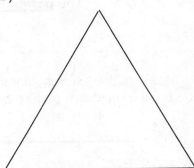

Perimeter = _____ triangles

c)

Perimeter = _____ triangles

Carlo makes a figure using toothpicks.

He counts the number of toothpicks around the outside of the figure:

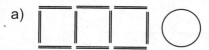 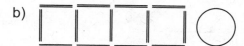 

| 1 | 2 | 3 | 4 | 5 | 6 |

The distance around the outside of a shape is called the **perimeter** of the shape.
The perimeter of Carlo's figure, measured in toothpicks, is <u>6 toothpicks</u>.

---

1. Count the number of toothpicks around the <u>outside</u> of the figure. (Mark the toothpicks as you count.)
   Write your answer in the circle provided.

   a) 　　　　b) 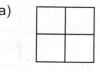　　　　c)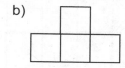

2. Count the number of edges around the <u>outside</u> of the figure, marking the edges as you count.

   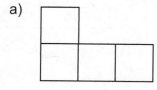 } edge

   a) 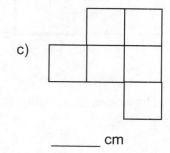　　　b)　　　c)

   _____　　　_____　　　_____

3. Each edge in the figure is 1 cm long. Find the perimeter in cm.

   a)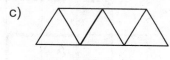

   _____ cm　　　b) _____ cm　　　c) _____ cm

4. The picture shows the designs for two swimming pools, marked in metres. Find the perimeter of
   each pool by writing an addition statement.

   a)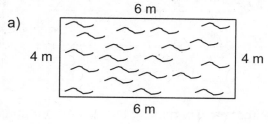

   b)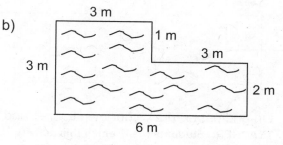

   _____　　　　_____

Measurement 1

ME3-13: Exploring Perimeter

1. Write the total length of each side beside the figure
   (one side is done for you).

   Then write an addition statement and find the perimeter.

   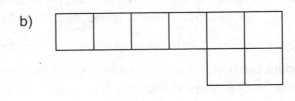

   2 cm

   Perimeter: _____

2. Write the total length of each side in cm as shown in the first figure.

   Then write an addition statement and find the perimeter. Don't miss any edges!

   a)

   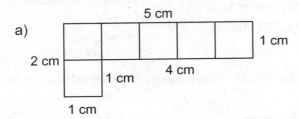

   5 cm

   2 cm

   1 cm

   1 cm

   4 cm

   1 cm

   Perimeter: _____

   b)

   Perimeter: _____

3. Each edge is 1 unit long. Write the length of each side beside the figure (don't miss any edges!).
   Then use the side lengths to find the perimeter.

   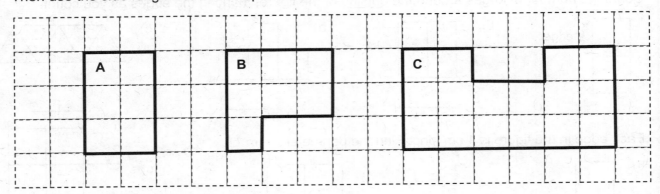

4. Draw your own figure and find the perimeter.

   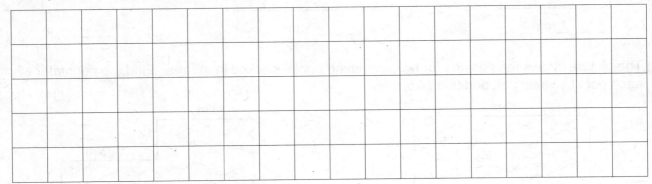

5. On grid paper, draw your own figures and find their perimeters. Try making letters or other shapes!
   **TEACHER: Students really enjoy this activity. Let them spend some time inventing shapes and then finding
   their perimeter.**

1. Estimate the perimeter of each shape in centimetres. (Use your finger or another object.)
   Then measure the perimeter with a ruler.

   a)

   Estimate = _____

   Perimeter = _____

   b)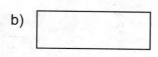

   Estimate = _____

   Perimeter = _____

   c)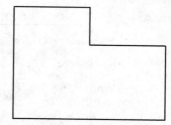

   Estimate = _____

   Perimeter = _____

2. Write the perimeter of each figure in the sequence (assume each edge is 1 unit).

   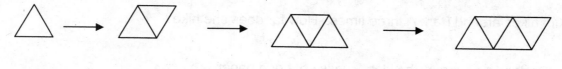

   _____   _____   _____   _____

   a) How does the perimeter change each time a triangle is added?

   _____

   b) If the sequence continued, what would the perimeter ...

      (i) of the 5th figure be? _____   (ii) of the 6th figure be? _____

3. a) Perimeter: _____

   Add one square so that
   the perimeter of the shape
   increases by 2:

   New Perimeter: _____

   b) Perimeter: _____

   Add one square so that
   the perimeter of the shape
   stays the same:

   New Perimeter: _____

4. The perimeter of the swimming pool is given. Find the missing side length.
   Explain how you found your answer.

   a)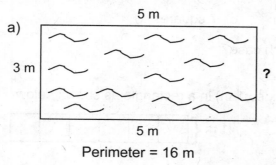

   b)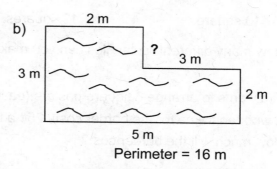

Answer the following questions in your notebook.

5. **Park A:**

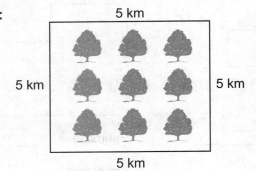

5 km
5 km
5 km
5 km

Park B:

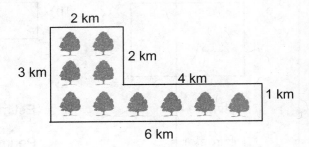

2 km
2 km
3 km
4 km
1 km
6 km

a) Kim hikes around the perimeter of Park A.
   Leslie hikes around Park B. Who hikes the furthest?

b) Kim hikes around Park A three times. How far does she hike?

6. Using a ruler draw a square with sides 3 units on a grid paper.
   Find the perimeter of the square.

7. How could you find the perimeter of a square with sides 5 cm without drawing a picture?

8. A square has perimeter 12 cm long.   What is the length of its side?

9. The picture shows two ways (A and B) to make a rectangle using 4 squares:

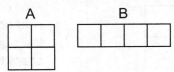

A   B

a) Which figure has the shorter perimeter? How do you know?

b) Are there any other ways to make a rectangle using 4 squares? Explain.

10. On grid paper, show all the ways you can make a rectangle using:

a) 10 squares   b) 12 squares   c) 7 squares

How many different rectangles can you make in each case?

11. Tim wants to arrange 6 square posters (each with sides 1 m) in a rectangle as shown below:
    A wooden frame for the border costs 25¢ a metre.
    How much will the border cost?

1 m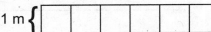

Mass measures the amount of matter, or substance, in a thing.

Grams (g) and **Kilograms** (kg) are units for measuring weight or mass.

One kilogram is equal to 1000 grams.

Things that weigh about one <u>gram</u>:
✓ A paper clip
✓ A dime
✓ A chocolate chip

Things that weigh about one <u>kilogram</u>:
✓ A 1-litre bottle of water
✓ A bag of 200 nickels
✓ A squirrel

---

1. Can you name an object that weighs about
   a) one gram? _____
   b) one kilogram? _____

2. Estimate the weight of the following things in …
   Grams:
   a) a chocolate chip cookie _____
   b) an apple _____
   c) a shoe _____
   Kilograms:
   d) your math book _____
   e) your school bag _____
   f) yourself _____

3. Match the objects on the left with objects on the right that have a similar weight.

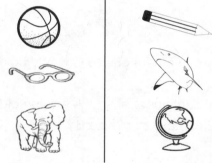

4. What unit is more appropriate to measure each item? Circle the appropriate unit.

 grams or **kilograms**?

 grams or **kilograms**?

 grams or **kilograms**?

5. a) How many dimes weigh as much as 6 nickels?
   b) How many quarters weigh as much as 5 nickels?

Coin	Weight
Dime	1 g
Nickel	4 g
Quarter	5 g

6. When Brian stands on a scale the arrow points to 40 kg.
   When he stands on the scale and holds his cat, the arrow points to 45 kg.
   How could he use these two measurements to find the weight of his cat?

ME3-16: Measuring Capacity

The **capacity** of a container is how much it can hold.

Litres and **millilitres** are units for measuring capacity.

✓ The capacity of a regular carton of juice is 1 litre:

One litre (L) equals 1000 millilitres (mL).

✓ A small glass holds almost 100 mL.

✓ A drop of water contains about 1 mL of water.

----

1. Which unit would you use to measure the capacity of the container.

   a)   L or mL?   b)   L or mL?

   c)  L or mL?   d)   L or mL?

2. Which set of containers has the greatest capacity? How do you know?

   a)

   OR

   b)

3.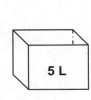

   2 L   **3 L**   **5 L**

   A   **B**   **C**

   a) How many containers of size C would hold 20 L?

   b) How many containers of size A would hold as much water as 2 containers of size B?

   c) Which will hold more, 4 containers of size B or 3 containers of size C?

4. How many containers would you need to make a litre if your container held ...

   a) 100 mL?   b) 200 mL?   c) 500 mL?   d) 250 mL?

5. To make punch for 6 people you need 50 mL of orange juice.
   How many mL of orange juice would you need to make punch for 12 people?
   Explain.

6. Clare fills a measuring cup with 40 mL of water.
   She pours out some water and notices there are 30 mL left.
   How much water did she pour out?

ME3-17: Measuring Temperature

Degree Celsius is a unit of measurement for temperature. It is written: °C

Water freezes at 0°C. Water boils at 100°C. The normal temperature of the human body is about 37°C.

1. Read the thermometers and record the temperature.

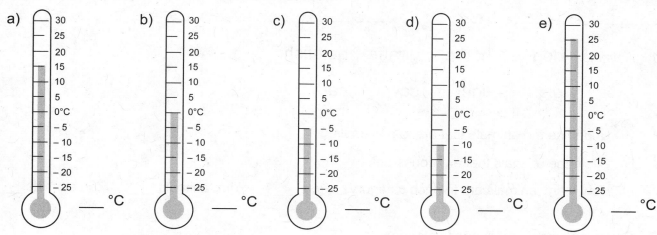

a) ____ °C   b) ____ °C   c) ____ °C   d) ____ °C   e) ____ °C

2. What is the normal temperature range of each season where you live? (Ask your teacher for help with this.)

a) Winter –
    between _____ °C and _____ °C

b) Spring –
    between _____ °C and _____ °C

c) Summer –
    between _____ °C and _____ °C

d) Fall –
    between _____ °C and _____ °C

3. Paul's temperature is 36°C.
    How much lower is his temperature than normal?

4. Jen heated some soup until it was boiling.
    She waited until its temperature was 40°C before she ate it.
    How much did the temperature change?

5. A lizard's body temperature can change from 15°C to 27°C.
    What is the difference between these two temperatures?

BONUS
6. Alana measured the temperature one day and found it was – 10°C.
    The next day, the temperature was 10°C. How many degrees did the temperature rise?

Measurement 1

Data is facts or information. For example, your age is a piece of data, and so is your name.

Data can be organized into **categories.**

We use **attributes** to sort data, such as:

• Gender (boy or girl)   • Age (age 9 or age 8)   • Length of Hair (long hair or short hair)

----

1. *Animals:* dog   horse   giraffe   goldfish

   pig   tiger   cow   cat

   a) Underline the animals that are zoo animals.

   b) Circle the animals that are house pets.

   c) How many animals are in each category?   Pets ____   Farm animals ____   Zoo animals ____

2. Count how many are in each category.

   Objects: coin   tree   window   telephone pole

   staple   newspaper   gold necklace

   Categories: Wood ____   Glass ____   Metal ____

3. Match the data with the correct category.

   A. carrot, lettuce, cucumber   ____ weather forecasts

   B. rainy, snowy, foggy   ____ tools

   C. morning, evening, noon   ____ vegetables

   D. hammer, wrench, saw   ____ times of day

4. Can you think of another piece of data for each category in Question 3?

   a) weather forecasts: _____

   b) tools: _____

   c) vegetables: _____

   d) times of day: _____

5. a)   Heather wants to sort her T-shirts into 2 categories: those <u>with</u> and those <u>without</u> patterns.

Here are her T-shirts. Notice that each has been given a letter.

Use the following table to help Heather sort her T-shirts.

Category	T-shirt (by letter)
T-shirts <u>with</u> pattern	A,
T-shirts <u>without</u> pattern	B,

How many patterned T-shirts does Heather have? _____

How many T-shirts without patterns does Heather have? _____

b)   Use the table below to sort Jessica's T-shirts.
NOTE: Some of Jessica's T-shirts are in more than one category.

T-shirt	A	B	C	D	E	F	G	H	I	J
dark colour		✓								
light colour	✓									
with pattern	✓									

How many T-shirts does Jessica have that are a dark colour AND have a pattern? _____

c)   Think of the T-shirts you own. What is a different way you could sort them?

Name the **categories** you would use to sort. _____

_____

_____

In math, we sometimes use circles to show which objects have a property.
Objects inside a circle have the property, and objects outside the circle do not.

- -

1. Put the letters from each shape inside or outside the circle. The first one is done for you.

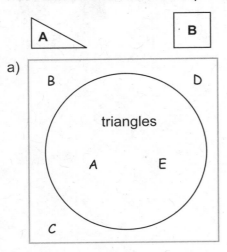

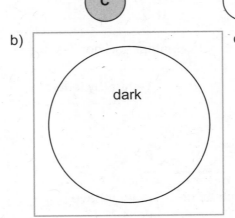

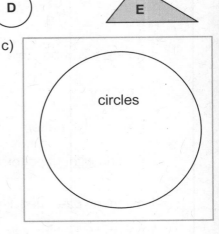

a)
```
B                    D

        triangles

     A          E

C
```

b) dark

c) circles

2. We can organize the shapes above into two circles at the same time.
   The overlapping circles are called a **Venn** diagram.

   a) Shade the area that is **inside** both circles.
      Put the correct letter in that area.

   b) Shade the area that is **outside** both circles.
      Put the correct letter in that area.

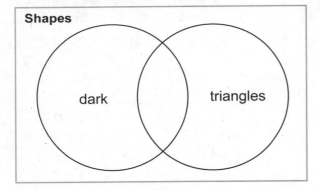

Shapes   dark   triangles

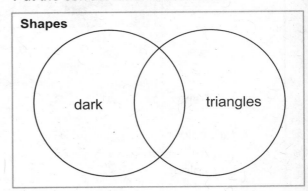

Shapes   dark   triangles

3. Complete the Venn diagrams.

   a)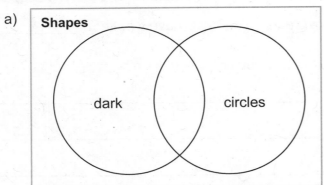

   Shapes   dark   circles

   b)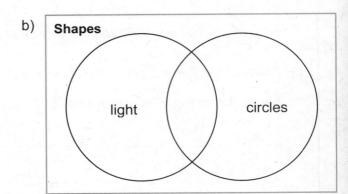

   Shapes   light   circles

Probability & Data Management 1

4. Complete the Venn diagram.

A. dog   **B. peacock**   **C. cat**   **D. goldfish**   **E. sparrow**   **F. spider**

Animals

has fur   has a tail

One part of the Venn diagram is empty. Explain what that means: _____

_____

Find an animal that goes into the empty part: _____

5. Complete the Venn diagrams.

a) A. rice   B. hat   C. sit   D. sat

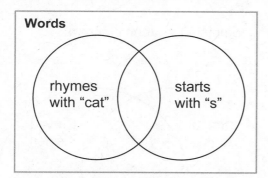

Words

rhymes with "cat"   starts with "s"

b) A. dog   B. fish   C. robin   D. clam

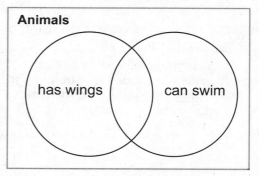

Animals

has wings   can swim

c) A. rat   B. rain   C. pot   D. sand

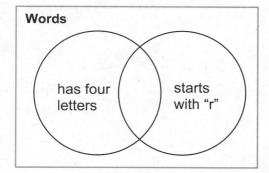

Words

has four letters   starts with "r"

d) A. Toronto   B. Canada   C. Manitoba   D. France

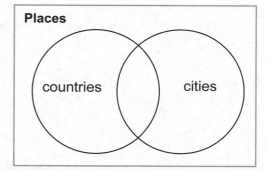

Places

countries   cities

6. Ian has a part-time job at a pet store.

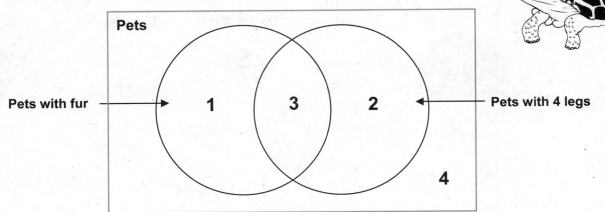

Pets

Pets with fur → 1   3   2 ← Pets with 4 legs

4

Help Ian classify these animals by giving the section of the Venn diagram where they belong.

Cat – [ ]　　　　Gerbil – [ ]　　　　Fish – [ ]

Dog – [ ]　　　　Lizard – [ ]　　　　Turtle – [ ]

7. Look at the following shapes:

 A　　 B　　 C　　 D　　 E　　 F

Complete the following table, then use the information to complete the Venn diagram.

Shape	Straight sides <u>only</u>	Curved sides <u>only</u>	Both straight <u>and</u> curved sides
A	✓		
B			
C			
D			
E			
F			

Shapes

Straight sides　　　　Curved sides

A

A **tally** is a useful way to record and count data. In a tally, each stroke represents 1.

| = 1 || = 2 ||| = 3 |||| = 4   ⊬⊬ = 5
⊬⊬ | = 6   ⊬⊬ || = 7   ⊬⊬ ||| = 8   ⊬⊬ |||| = 9   ⊬⊬ ⊬⊬ = 10

Every fifth stroke is made sideways. This makes it easy to use skip counting by 5s to count a tally:

⊬⊬ ⊬⊬ ⊬⊬ ⊬⊬ ⊬⊬ ⊬⊬ ||
5   10 15 20 25 30 32

---

1. Provide the number that matches the given tally. The first one has been done for you.

   a) ||| = __3__   b) ⊬⊬ = ____   c) || = ____

   d) |||| = ____   e) ⊬⊬ |||| = ____   f) ⊬⊬ ||| = ____

   g) | = ____   h) ⊬⊬ | = ____   i) ⊬⊬ || = ____

   j) ⊬⊬ ⊬⊬ || = ____   k) ⊬⊬ ⊬⊬ ⊬⊬ = ____

   l) ⊬⊬ ⊬⊬ ⊬⊬ ⊬⊬ = ____   m) ⊬⊬ ⊬⊬ ⊬⊬ ||| = ____

2. Provide the tally that matches the given number.

   a) 5 = ⊬⊬   b) 2 =   c) 6 =

   d) 8 =   e) 4 =   f) 1 =

   g) 7 =   h) 9 =   i) 3 =

   j) 20 =   k) 12 =

   l) 16 =   m) 27 =

3. What is your favourite number between 1 and 30?
   Draw the matching tally.

1. A teacher did a survey of her students' favourite fruits. Here is a tally of the responses:

Apples	Bananas	Oranges	Grapes	Peaches	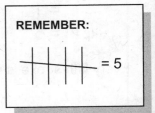 REMEMBER: ∦ = 5
ℍ ⫴	ℍ ℍ	ℍ ∣	∣∣∣∣	∣∣∣	
7	_____	_____	_____	_____	

a) Fill in the blanks in the chart by counting the tally results.

b) How many students like oranges best? _____

c) How many students like grapes best? _____

> You can **compare** and **order** the data for each fruit to find new information.

d) Which fruit was the *most* popular? _____

e) Which fruit was the *least* popular? _____

f) Did more students like oranges best or grapes best? _____

g) List the fruits in order, from *most* popular to *least* popular.

_____

> You can **add** data from the chart to find new information.

2. a) How many students were in the class? _____

b) Altogether, how many students liked apples *or* bananas best? _____

> You can **subtract** data from the chart to find new information.

3. a) How many more students liked bananas best than peaches best? _____

b) How many students did not choose bananas? _____
   HINT: Use your answer from 2 a).

> You can **multiply** data from the chart to find new information.

c) What fruit is twice as popular as peaches? _____

 jump math

Probability & Data Management 1

A **pictograph** uses a **symbol** to represent data.

Number of Books Read in December	
Ravi	📖 📖 📖 📖 📖
Kamal	📖 📖 📖

The scale of the pictograph is the number of items each symbol represents.

A **key** tells what the scale is.

Number of Books Read in 1 Year	
Ravi	📖 📖 📖 📖 📖
Kamal	📖 📖 📖
1 📖 means 10 books	

OR

Key to the scale

Number of Books Read in 1 Year	
Ravi	📖 📖 📖 📖 📖 📖 📖 📖 📖 📖
Kamal	📖 📖 📖 📖 📖
1 📖 means 5 books	

- -

1. Using the pictograph given below, answer the following questions.

SCALE: 1💧 = 1 day of rain

Month	Number of Rainy Days	Count
April	💧 💧 💧 💧 💧 💧 💧 💧	
May	💧 💧 💧 💧 💧	
June	💧 💧 💧 💧	
July	💧 💧 💧	
August	💧 💧 💧 💧	

a) How many rainy days were there in July? _____ in May? _____

b) Which month had 3 rainy days? _____

c) Which month was the rainiest? _____

d) Which months had the same number of rainy days? _____

e) June has 30 days. On how many days in June was there no rain? _____

   How do you know? _____

f) Describe 2 other things you can tell from reading this pictograph.

Manuel has counted the flowers in his garden.

Flower	Daffodil	Buttercup	Daisy
Number	15	25	40

He wants to display his data in a pictograph.

Here are two ways he could display his data, using a **scale**.

Number of Flowers

Daffodil ✻ ✻ ✻
Buttercup ✻ ✻ ✻ ✻ ✻
Daisy ✻ ✻ ✻ ✻ ✻ ✻ ✻ ✻
Scale: One ✻ means 5 flowers

Number of Flowers

Daffodil ◯◖
Buttercup ◯◯◖
Daisy ◯◯◯◯
Scale: One ◯ means 10 flowers

---

1. a) If one ◯ means 5 people, then …

   i) ◯◯◯◯ means _____ people.
   ii) ◯◯◯ means _____ people.

   iii) ◯◯◯◯◯◯◯◯ means _____ people.

   b) If one ✻ means 2 flowers, then …

   i) ✻ ✻ ✻ ✻ means _____ flowers.
   ii) ✻ ✻ ✻ ✻ ✻ means _____ flowers.

   iii) ✻ ✻ ✻ ✻ ✻ ✻ ✻ ✻ ✻ means _____ flowers.

   c) If one ▢ means 3 boxes, then …

   i) ▢▢▢ means _____ boxes.
   ii) ▢▢ means _____ boxes.

   iii) ▢▢▢▢ means _____ boxes.
   iv) ▢▢▢▢▢▢ means _____ boxes.

2. Lisa forgot to draw some circles in her pictograph. Fill in the missing circles.

   1 ◯ means 5 students

Grade	Number of Students in Each Grade	Pictograph
3	┼┼┼┼ ┼┼┼┼ ┼┼┼┼ ┼┼┼┼ ┼┼┼┼	◯◯◯◯◯
4	┼┼┼┼ ┼┼┼┼ ┼┼┼┼ ┼┼┼┼ ┼┼┼┼ ┼┼┼┼	◯◯◯◯
5	┼┼┼┼ ┼┼┼┼ ┼┼┼┼ ┼┼┼┼	◯◯

 jump math
MULTIPLYING POTENTIAL

Probability & Data Management 1

3. In the line plot below, each ✗ represents 2 students.

   Redraw the line plot so that each ✗ represents 4 students.

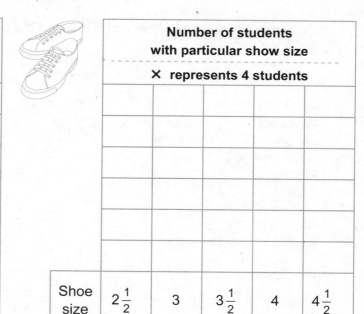

Number of students with a particular shoe size				
✗ represents 2 students				
		✗		
		✗		
	✗	✗	✗	
	✗	✗	✗	
✗	✗	✗	✗	✗
✗	✗	✗	✗	✗

| Shoe size | $2\frac{1}{2}$ | 3 | $3\frac{1}{2}$ | 4 | $4\frac{1}{2}$ |

Number of students with particular show size				
✗ represents 4 students				

| Shoe size | $2\frac{1}{2}$ | 3 | $3\frac{1}{2}$ | 4 | $4\frac{1}{2}$ |

4. a) If ◯ means 4 people then ◖ means _____ people.

    b) If ◯ means 6 people then ◖ means _____ people.

    c) If ◯ means 10 people then ◖ means _____ people.

    d) If ◯ means 14 people then ◖ means _____ people.

    e) If ◯ means 20 people then ◖ means _____ people.

5. If one ◯ means 10 people then …

    a) ◯ ◯ ◖ means _____ people.   b) ◯ ◯ ◯ ◖ means _____ people.

    c) ◯ ◯ ◯ ◯ ◯ ◯ ◯ ◖ means _____ people.

6. Which scale is best for the data?

    a) 12, 6, 8   ☐ scale of 2   ☐ scale of 5   ☐ scale of 10

    b) 30, 90, 60   ☐ scale of 2   ☐ scale of 5   ☐ scale of 10

    c) 9, 12, 6   ☐ scale of 2   ☐ scale of 3   ☐ scale of 5

    d) 25, 10, 35   ☐ scale of 2   ☐ scale of 3   ☐ scale of 5

7. For one set of data in Question 6 explain why you chose the scale.

PDM3-7: Displaying Data on a Pictograph

1. Antoine surveyed his classmates to find out which primary colour they liked best.

   a) Use Antoine's tally to find how many of his classmates liked each colour best.

   b) Choose your own symbol and complete the pictograph.

1 _____ means 3 classmates

Favourite Colour	Number of Classmates	Count	Favourite Primary Colour *Make the pictograph here.*
Blue	☰☰☰☰ IIII	9	
Red	☰☰☰☰ ☰☰☰☰ II		
Yellow	☰☰☰☰ I		

2. Brianna counted the number of students in each grade at her school. Complete her pictograph.

1 ☺ = 5 students

Grade	Number of Students	Count	Number of Students in Each Grade *Make the pictograph here.*
3	☰☰☰☰ ☰☰☰☰ ☰☰☰☰ ☰☰☰☰ ☰☰☰☰ ☰☰☰☰ ☰☰☰☰ ☰☰☰☰		
4	☰☰☰☰ ☰☰☰☰ ☰☰☰☰ ☰☰☰☰ ☰☰☰☰		
5	☰☰☰☰ ☰☰☰☰ ☰☰☰☰ ☰☰☰☰ ☰☰☰☰ ☰☰☰☰ ☰☰☰☰		

3. Create a pictograph of Brianna's data using a scale of: 1 _____ means 10 students.
   HINT: Pick your symbol carefully!

A **bar graph** has 4 parts:

- a vertical and a horizontal **axis**,
- a **scale**,
- **labels** (including a title),
- and **data** (shown in bars).

The bars in a bar graph can be vertical or horizontal.

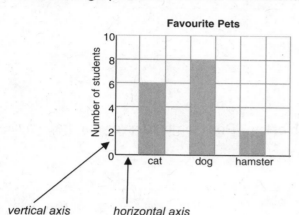

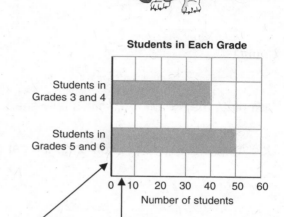

The labels tell what the data in the bar is.

The scale tells how much each division of the grid represents.

---

1. The graph shows the hair colour of the students in a Grade 3 class.

   a) How many students have …

      black hair? _____

      blonde hair? _____

   b) 5 students in the class have brown hair.
      Colour the final bar in the graph to show this.

   c) How many students
      <u>don't</u> have black hair? _____

   d) How many more students
      have brown hair than red hair? _____

   e) Altogether, how many
      students are there in the class? _____

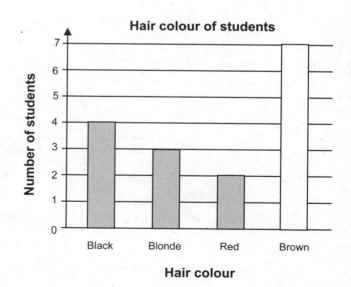

2. Anita did a survey of the birds she saw in a park.
   Here are her results.

Bird Type	Sparrows	Robins	Pigeons	Blue Jays
Tally	||||| ||	||||	||||| |||||	||
Count				

a) Complete the "count" on Anita's tally chart.

b) Use Anita's tally chart to complete the bar graph below. Don't forget to give your graph a title!

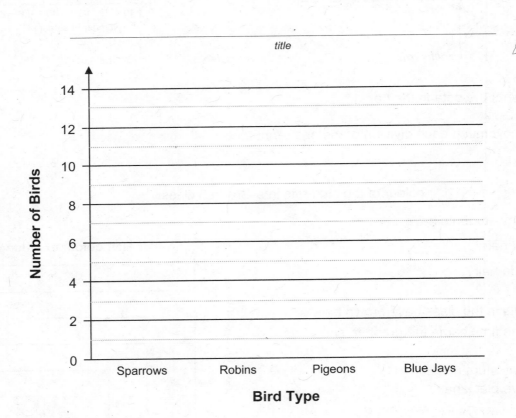

title

c) What are two conclusions Anita could draw from her data?

● _____

● _____

1.

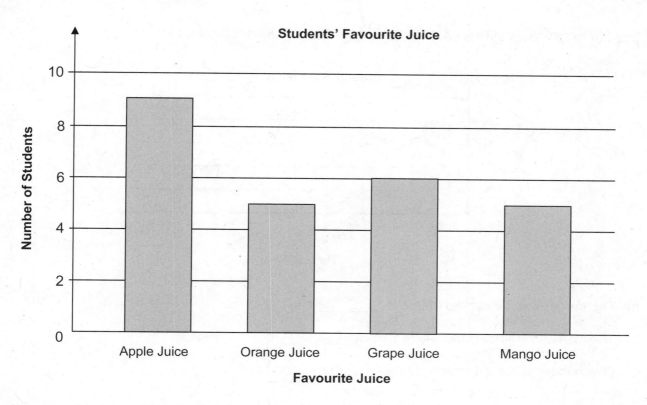

Students' Favourite Juice

a) What was the most popular juice? _____

b) Which two juices were preferred by the same number of students?

_____

c) If the teacher could bring two kinds of juice on a field trip, which kinds should he or she bring?

_____

2. The students in a Grade 3 class collected coats for charity.

They collected …

- Two times as many coats in January as in December.

- 3 more coats in February than in December

- 15 coats altogether.

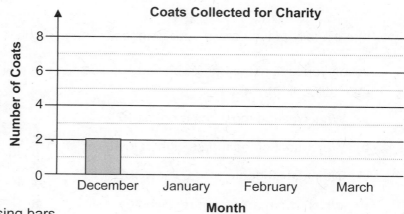

a) Use the clues above to fill in the missing bars.

b) Write three conclusions you could draw from the bar graph.

3. This bar graph gives the snowfall for Guelph (in cm) at different times of the year.

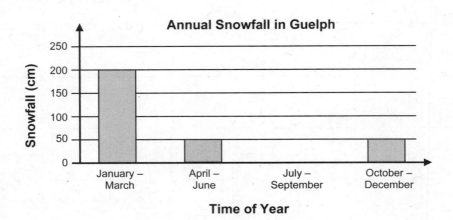

Annual Snowfall in Guelph

a) The snowfall in January to March is _____ cm.

b) The total snowfall over the whole year is _____ cm.

c) Which months have no bar? Explain why there is no bar.

_____

4. The following students wrote a spelling test. Their marks (out of 20) were:

Adam	10	Akeila	15	Joanne	20	Shey	20
Ben	10	Fabiola	15	Beth	20	Sally	5
Kim	20	Rosa	10	Sahar	20	Imran	20
Jenny	15	Abdul	20	Ken	5	Noomph	20
Shawn	15	Cesar	10	Sharla	15	Aidan	10

Make a tally of the data in your notebook. Then complete the bar graph.

When you look at the bar graph you can see the <u>shape</u> of the data.

a) What was the most common mark?

b) Were most of the marks high or low?

c) Did most students score below 15?

d) Which two marks were received by the same number of students?

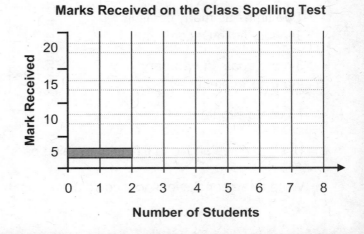

Marks Received on the Class Spelling Test

1.

Jesse has a pet parakeet at home and loves animals. He also has a new baby sister! So, for his school project, he chose the topic "Zoo Animals and Their Babies".

He called the local zoo and got the following information from the zookeeper.

Data Chart 1

Animal	Number of Babies Born to a Female
Siberian Tiger	1
Black Bear	2
River Otter	3
Red Fox	5
Coyote	7

Data Chart 2

Animal	Number of Adult Females That Had Babies in 2004
Siberian Tiger	1
Black Bear	2
River Otter	3
Red Fox	2
Coyote	1

a) Complete his chart.

Animal	Number of Babies Born at the Zoo in 2004
Siberian Tiger	____ × ____ = ____
Black Bear	
River Otter	
Red Fox	
Coyote	

b) Create a bar graph to display the information on the number of babies born at the zoo in 2004. Think carefully about the scale you choose.

✓ Data you collect yourself is called **first-hand data**:

Some ways you can collect first-hand data are by:

- measuring items
- conducting an experiment
- conducting a survey.

✓ Data collected by someone else is called **second-hand data**.

You can find second-hand data in books and magazines, and on the Internet.

Writing a Survey Question

1. Decide what you want to know. (For example, "What is the favourite fruit of my classmates?")

2. The question should not have too many responses.
One of the responses could be "other."

Example:

What is your favourite fruit?

✗ This question may give you too many answers.

What fruit do you like?
☐ apples ☐ grapes ☐ oranges ☐ other?

✗ This question is not worded precisely. People could give more than one answer.

Which is your favourite fruit?
☐ apples ☐ grapes ☐ oranges ☐ other?

✓ This <u>is</u> a better survey question.

1. Write a survey question to find out what pizza toppings students like best.

_____

_____ ?

☐ _____   ☐ _____   ☐ _____

☐ _____   ☐ _____   ☐ other?

2. Write a different survey question you could ask your classmates.

_____

_____

_____

Probability & Data Management 1

RECAP

Here are the steps to planning a survey:

Decide … i) **What** you want to know. ii) **Who** you will survey and **how many** people you will survey.

iii) **When** and **where** you will conduct your survey. iv) **How** you will record your data.

Then **write** your survey question, **predict** what the response to your survey will be, and **conduct** your survey. Were the results of your survey what you expected?

Before you make up your own survey, practice with the one below.

1. a) Survey your classmates to find out their favourite subjects. Use the following table to tally and count your results.

Subject Area	Tally	Count
Math		
Gym		
French		
Reading		
Writing		
_____		
_____		
_____		
_____		

b) What scale (i.e. counting by 1s, 2s, 3s, 5s, 10s, etc.) would be the best for a bar graph of your data? Why?

c) Using the scale you've picked, create a bar graph of the data you collected.
Don't forget to add numbers along the axes. Also include a good title.

title

Number of students

Favourite subject area

d) List three conclusions you can draw from your bar graph.

- _____

- _____

- _____

PDM3-13: Blank Tally Chart and Bar Graph

1. Make up your own survey. Use the chart and grid below to record and display the data you collect.
   NOTE: On your bar graph, remember to include a title, labels, and the scale.

Question: _____

Categories	Tally	Count

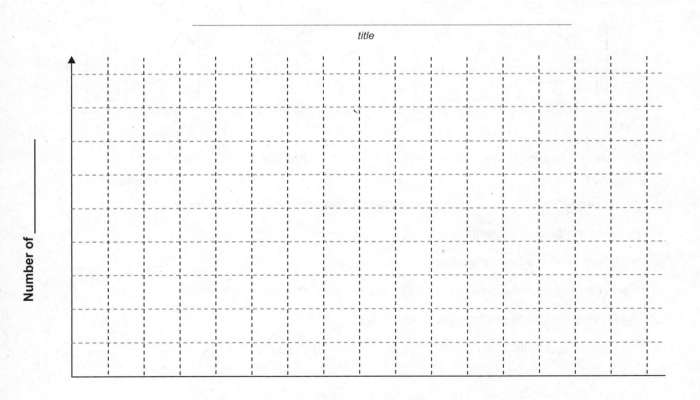

title

Number of ____

Answer the questions below in your notebook.

1. Tim asked the Grade 3 students in his school about their favourite animal.
   Here are the results of the survey.

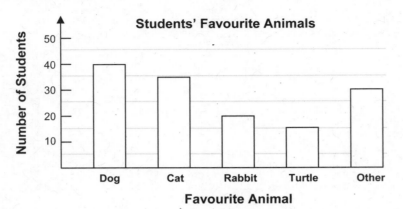

Give some information you can find from the graph by ....

• **Comparing**   • **Ordering**   • **Adding**   • **Subtracting**   • **Multiplying**   • **Dividing Data**

2. Each bar graph represents the favourite sports of Grade 3 students.
   Find the missing numbers on the bars.

a)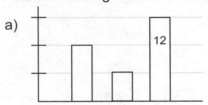

b)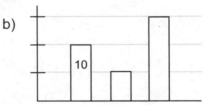

c)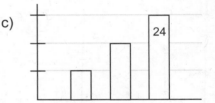

3. In each case, say which method you would you use to find the data ...

   • **a survey?**   • **measuring?**   • **counting?**

   • **an experiment?**   • **researching in books or on the Internet?**

   a) How far students can jump.

   b) How fast different animals can run.

   c) How many students in your class have each colour of hair.

   d) The favourite sports of students in your class.

   e) How many students can count to 100 in 1 minute or less.

4. Collect and display your own data. Here are some suggestions:

   • **distance class members can jump**   • **weight of your textbooks**

   • **types of birds that live in your area**   • **favourite animals or sports**

Shapes, such as triangles and squares, have **sides** (or 'edges') and **vertices** ('corners' where the sides meet).

A flat shape is called a 2-dimensional (or 2-D) shape.

A **polygon** is a 2-D shape with sides that are all straight lines.

Example: vertices ⟶   ⟵ side

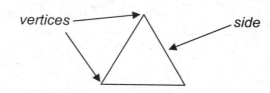

<u>SIDES</u>

Tim marks the sides of a shape as he counts so he does not miss any sides.

Example:

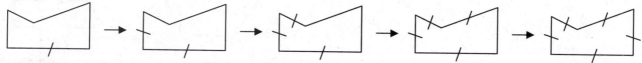

This shape has **5** sides.

----

1. Use Tim's method to find the number of sides on each shape.

a)

____ sides

b)

____ sides

c)

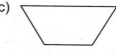

____ sides

d)

____ sides

2. Helen names the shapes according to how many sides they have.

a) triangle

____ sides

b) quadrilateral

____ sides

c) pentagon

____ sides

d) hexagon

____ sides

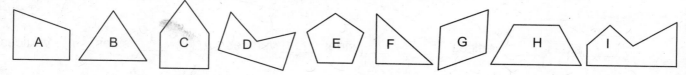

3. Complete the chart. Find as many shapes as you can for each shape name.

Shapes	Letters
Triangles	
Quadrilaterals	

Shapes	Letters
Pentagons	
Hexagons	

G3-1: Sides and Vertices *(continued)*

<u>VERTICES</u>
Tim puts a circle around each vertex as he counts so he doesn't miss any vertices.

Example:

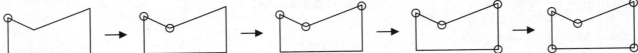

This shape has **5** vertices.

- -

4. Use Tim's method to find the number of vertices on each shape.

a)
____ vertices

b)
____ vertices

c)
____ vertices

d)
____ vertices

5. Find the number of sides and vertices in each of the following polygons.

a)
____ sides ____ vertices

b)
____ sides ____ vertices

c)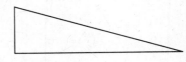
____ sides ____ vertices

d)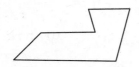
____ sides ____ vertices

e)
____ sides ____ vertices

f)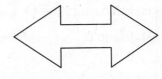
____ sides ____ vertices

g)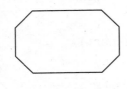
____ sides ____ vertices

h)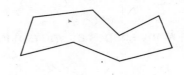
____ sides ____ vertices

i)
____ sides ____ vertices

 BONUS

6. Can you draw a polygon in which the number of sides <u>does not equal</u> the number of vertices?

7. How many sides does a stop sign have? Ask your teacher the name of this shape.

Manuel and his class are learning about angles. To show them angles of different sizes, Manuel's teacher first folds a piece of paper in half.

 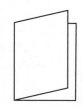 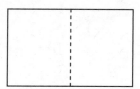

She then shows her students the side view of the folded piece of paper, opening it different amounts to represent different sized angles.

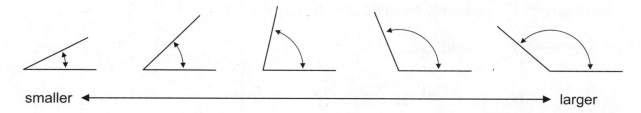

smaller ←――――――――――――――――――――――――――――――→ larger

Right angles (or <u>square</u> <u>corners</u>) appear in many places, including the corners of squares, rectangles and some triangles.

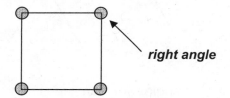 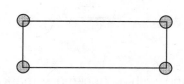

Manuel's teacher shows the class how to use the corner of a piece of paper to see if an angle is a **right angle**.

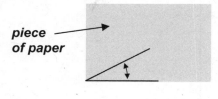 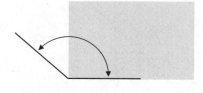 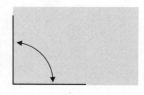

　　　<u>NOT</u> a right angle　　　　　<u>NOT</u> a right angle　　　　a <u>RIGHT ANGLE</u>

1.　Circle the angles that are **right angles**.
　　HINT: You can check with the corner of a piece of paper.

　　a)　　　　　　　　b)　　　　　　　　c)　　　　　　　　d)

 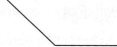 

e)   f)  g)   h)

i)   j)   k)   l)

2. Circle all the **right angles** in the following shapes.
   Then, inside each shape, write the number of right angles it has.

a)
   4

b)

c)

d)

e)

f)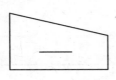

g)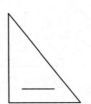

h)

3. Look at the picture below and, with a checkmark, mark all the right angles you can find.

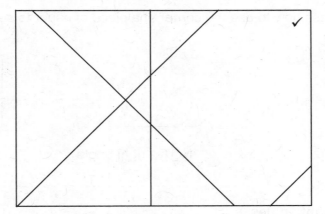

4. On grid paper (or a geoboard), create a shape with <u>four</u> sides and …

   a) no right angles   b) four right angles   c) two right angles   d) one right angle

5. List all the right angles you can see in your classroom (e.g. the corner of a door).

A polygon with all sides the same length is called **equilateral**. ("Equi" comes from a Latin word meaning "equal" and "lateral" means "sides.")

To find out if a shape is equilateral, Betsey uses her ruler to measure its sides.

Example:

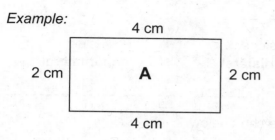

4 cm

2 cm **A** 2 cm

4 cm

3 cm

3 cm **B** 3 cm

3 cm

Shape A is **not** equilateral.

Shape B **is** equilateral.

NOTE: All squares are equilateral.

- -

1. Using your ruler, measure the sides of the shapes below. Circle those that are equilateral.

a)

_____ cm   _____ cm

_____ cm

b)

_____ cm   _____ cm

_____ cm   _____ cm

_____ cm

c)

_____ cm

_____ cm   _____ cm

_____ cm

d)

_____ cm

_____ cm   _____ cm

_____ cm

2. Can you name the polygons in Question 1? Write the name under each shape.

3. Based on the properties of the following figures, fill in the chart below.

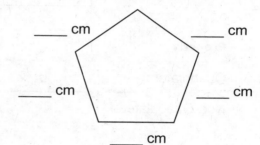

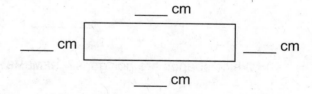

Property	Shape with Property
Equilateral	
Non-Equilateral	

G3-4: Quadrilaterals and Other Polygons

A polygon with four sides is called a **quadrilateral**.   *Example:*

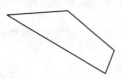

| 3 sides | 4 sides | 4 sides | 4 sides |
| NOT a quadrilateral | **quadrilateral** | **quadrilateral** | **quadrilateral** |

----

1.   Based on the properties of the following figures, fill in the chart below.

  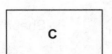

  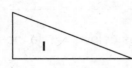

Property	Shape with Property
Quadrilateral	
Non-Quadrilateral	

2.

a) Which shapes are polygons? **REMEMBER: A polygon has straight sides.** _____

b) Which shapes are equilateral? _____

c) Which shapes have at least one curved side? _____

d) What do shapes D and E have in common? _____

e) What do shapes B, C and G have in common? _____

_____

f) Which shape doesn't belong in this group: A, B, C and G? Explain. _____

_____

Special Quadrilaterals: Some quadrilaterals have specific names. You can identify these special quadrilaterals by the particular properties they have.

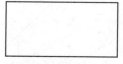
Rectangle
quadrilateral with
4 right angles

Square
quadrilateral with equal sides
and 4 right angles

Rhombus
quadrilateral with
equal sides

A **square** is a rectangle (because it has 4 right angles) *and* a rhombus (because its sides are all equal).

- -

3. For each of the quadrilaterals below, circle the **right angles**.
   Then measure the length of each side with a ruler and write it in the blank provided.
   Then name the quadrilateral.

a) _____ cm
_____ cm   _____ cm
_____ cm

_____

b) _____ cm
_____ cm   _____ cm
_____ cm

_____

c) _____ cm
_____ cm   _____ cm
_____ cm

_____

4. Using the figures below, complete the two charts. Start by circling the right angles in each figure.

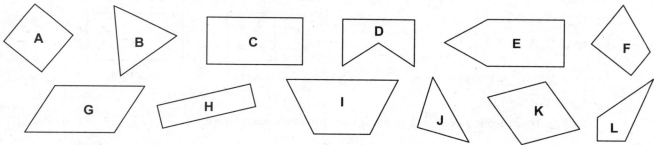

a)

Property	Shapes with Property
No right angles	
1 right angle	
2 right angles	
4 right angles	

b)

Property	Shapes with Property
Quadrilaterals	
Rectangles	
Rhombuses	
Squares	

5. Describe any similarities and differences between a rhombus and a square.

6. a) Why is a square a rectangle?   b) Why aren't all rectangles squares?

G3-5: Tangrams

A **tangram** is an ancient Chinese puzzle. The tangram is a square divided into seven pieces called tans.

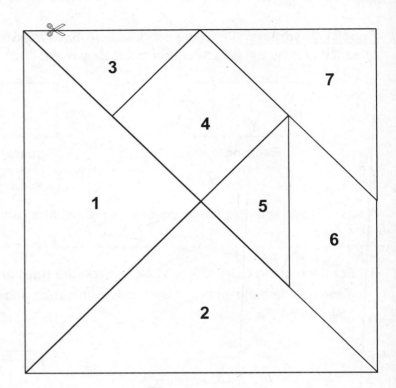

TEACHER:
You will need to have a set of tangrams or a photocopy of this page for each student.
Students may need help cutting out the shapes.
(It is important that the shapes are cut accurately.)

REMEMBER:
A shape with 5 sides is a <u>pentagon</u> and a shape with 6 sides is a <u>hexagon</u>.

---

1. Which tans are …

   a) quadrilaterals? _____

   b) triangles? _____

2. You can make a square and a rectangle using tans.

   Make a <u>square</u> using …

   a) tans 1 and 2.

   b) tans 3, 5, and 7.

   Make a <u>rectangle</u> using …

   c) tans 3, 4 and 5.

   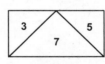

   square   *rectangle*

   NOTE: Trace around your tans to show how you made each figure.

   BONUS
3. Make a pentagon from tans 3, 4, 5 and 7.

4. Predict the shapes that you can make using the tans listed (copy and complete the chart).

Tan Pieces	Predicted Shapes Possible	Shapes Made
3 and 5		
3, 5 and 6		
4 and 6		

5. Can you combine some of your tangram pieces to make pictures that look like these?

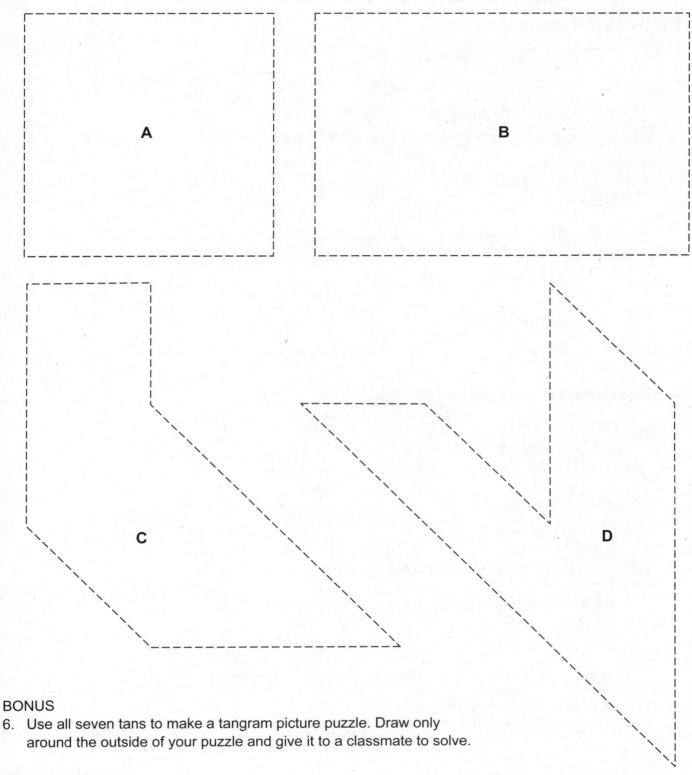

BONUS

6. Use all seven tans to make a tangram picture puzzle. Draw only around the outside of your puzzle and give it to a classmate to solve.

IMPORTANT NOTE:
Keep your tans in a safe place! You will need them for other lessons.

Shapes are **congruent** if they are the **same size _and_ shape**.
NOTE: Shapes are still called congruent if they are rotated and flipped.

These pairs of shapes are congruent.

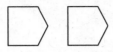 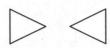 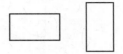

----

1. Write <u>congruent</u> or <u>not congruent</u> under each pair of shapes.

a)

not congruent

b)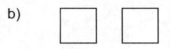

c)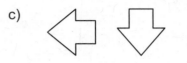

d)

e)

f)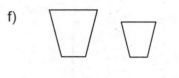

2. Circle the pairs of shapes that are congruent.

a)

b)

c)

d)

3. Again, circle the pair of shapes that are congruent.

a)

b)

c)

d)

e)

f)

Congruent shapes can be different colours or shades. These pairs of shapes are congruent:

---

1. Circle the pairs of shapes that are congruent.

a)   b)

c)   d)

2. There are 6 <u>pairs</u> of congruent shapes below. Show each pair by labelling them the <u>same number</u>.

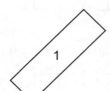    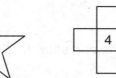

  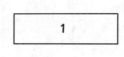

3. Write "congruent" or "not congruent" under each pair of shapes.
    REMEMBER: Two shapes are congruent if they have the same size and shape.

a)   b) 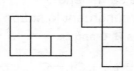   c)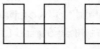

_____   _____   _____

4. Are these pairs of shapes congruent?

a) _____ because _____

_____

b)   _____ because _____

_____

1. Circle the two shapes that are congruent.
   REMEMBER: Colour doesn't matter!

   a) 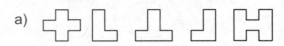   b)

   c) 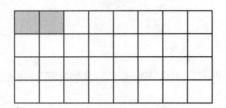   d)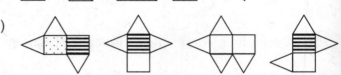

2. Draw a rectangle <u>congruent</u> to the one shown.

   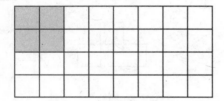

3. Draw a square congruent to the one shown.

   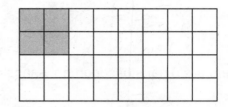

4. Draw a square NOT congruent to the one shown.

   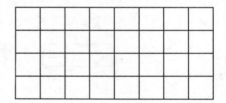

5. Draw two triangles that are NOT congruent.

6. Label any congruent shapes with the same letter.
   (Start by finding two shapes that are congruent to shape A.)
   HINT: You will also need to use the letters B, C and D.

   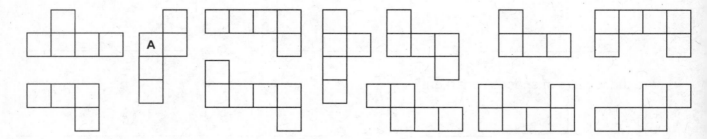

BONUS

7. Name two congruent shapes in your classroom. How can you check they are congruent?

_____

_____

1. Make a congruent copy of the shape on dot paper or on a geoboard.
    Draw your shape below.

a) 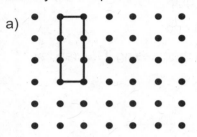   b) 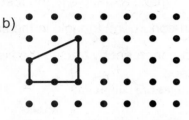   c)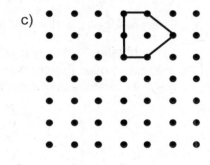

2. Make a copy of the shape **but** make your shape point **upwards**, rather than sideways.
    Draw your shape below.

a) 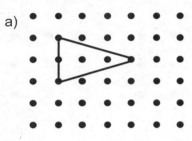   b) 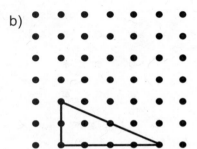   c)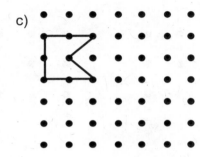

3. List the pairs of shapes that are congruent in the chart below.
    NOTE: One of the shapes is NOT congruent to any other shapes.

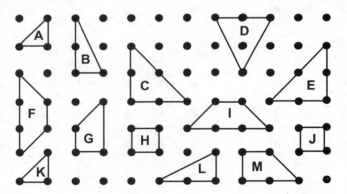

Congruent Shapes
Example: A and K

BONUS

4. This is a game for two people.

    You will need: two geoboards, two elastic bands and a partner.

    *   Player One: Make a quadrilateral on your geoboard with the elastic band.

    *   Tell your partner how to make the shape.
        (How tall is it? Does it have a right angle? How wide is the base?)

    *   Compare your shape to your partner's shape. Are they congruent? (How can you check?)

G3-10: Exploring Congruency with Grids

Sean is investigating how many non-congruent triangles he can make on a 3 x 3 grid of dots.

- Using a ruler, he joins 3 dots to make a triangle in the first 3 x 3 grid.

- Then he draws a different (non-congruent) triangle in the second grid.

- Sean checks that they are non-congruent by tracing the first and then seeing if he can lay the shape over the second shape.
  HINT: Be careful – all of these triangles are congruent!

If you end up making congruent triangles, shade them the same colour.

BONUS
Try finding some different quadrilaterals or pentagons.

Some shapes have lines of **symmetry**. Tina places a mirror across half the shape. If the half reflected in the mirror makes the shape 'whole' again, then the shape is symmetrical.

Tina also checks if a shape has a line of symmetry by cutting out the shape and then folding it. If the halves of the shapes on either side of the fold match exactly, the fold shows a **line of symmetry**.

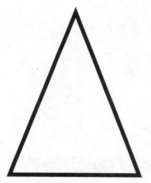

----

1. Trace and then cut each of the figures below.
   Fold the figure to show the line of symmetry.
   With a ruler, draw the line of symmetry on the original picture below.

a) 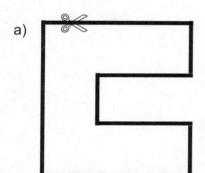   b)   c)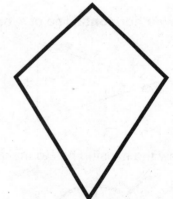

2. Each of these shapes has <u>more than one</u> line of symmetry. Again, trace, cut out and fold the figures to find the lines of symmetry and then draw the lines of symmetry onto the original picture.

a) 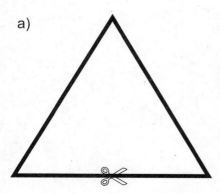   b)    c)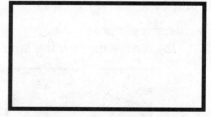

G3-12: Lines of Symmetry

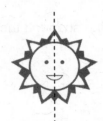

This picture has a
vertical line of symmetry.

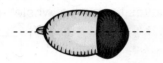

This picture has a
horizontal line of symmetry.

---

1. Draw a **vertical** line of symmetry onto the pictures with a ruler.

a)

b)

c)

2. Draw a **horizontal** line of symmetry with a ruler.

a)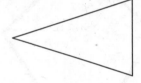

b)

c)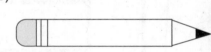

3. Draw the missing half to make each picture symmetrical.

a)

b)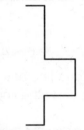

c)

4. These pictures have <u>more than one line of symmetry</u>.
   Use a ruler to draw the lines of symmetry onto the pictures.

a)

b)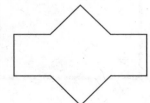

c)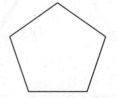

Geometry 1

G3-13: Completing Symmetric Shapes

1. Draw the missing half of the image to make the picture symmetrical.

a) 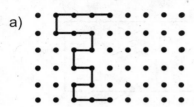   b)    c)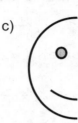

d) 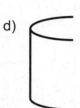   e)    f)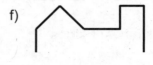

2. Draw the missing half so that the picture has two lines of symmetry. Draw both lines of symmetry.

a) 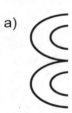   b) 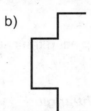   c)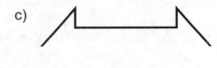

3. Draw a line on a piece of paper. Make the design on one side of the line using pattern blocks. Then make a mirror image of the design on the other side of the line.

a) 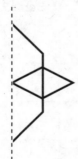   b) 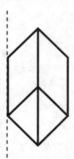   c)

4. There are symmetrical objects everywhere.
   Draw some objects that have a line of symmetry.
   Draw their line(s) of symmetry too.

G3-14: Comparing Shapes

1. a) Compare the two shapes by completing the following chart.

Square

Rectangle

Property	Square	Rectangle	Same?	Different?
Number of **vertices**	4	4	✓	
Number of **sides**	4	4		
Number of **right angles**	4	4		
At least one line of **symmetry**?	Yes	Yes		
More than one line of **symmetry**?	Yes	Yes		
Is the figure **equilateral**?	Yes	No		

b) As above, compare these two shapes by completing the chart.

Equilateral Triangle

Right-angled Triangle

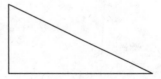

Property	Equilateral Triangle	Right-angled Triangle	Same?	Different?
Number of **vertices**				
Number of **sides**				
Number of **right angles**				
Any lines of **symmetry**?				
Number of lines of **symmetry**?				
Is the figure **equilateral**?				

c) By simply looking at the following figures, can you say how they are the same and different?

Right-angled Triangle

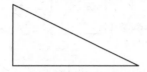

Rectangle

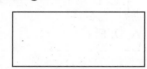

Property	Same?	Different?
Number of **vertices**		
Number of **sides**		
Number of **right angles**		
Any lines of **symmetry**?		
Number of lines of **symmetry**?		
Is the figure **equilateral**?		

2. Looking at the following figures, can you comment on their similarities (things that are the same) and differences?

Be sure to mention the following properties:

✓ The number of **vertices**

✓ The number of **sides**

✓ The number of **right angles**

✓ Lines of **symmetry**

✓ Number of lines of **symmetry**

✓ Whether the figure is **equilateral**

Pentagon

Hexagon

Similarities:	Differences:

3. Describe any similarities and differences between each pair of shapes.

a)

b)

c)

The following figures can be sorted by their properties using a Venn diagram:

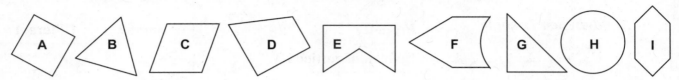

1. a)

Property	Figures with this property:
1. Quadrilateral	A, C, D
2. Has 2 or more right angles	A, D, E, I

Which figures share both properties? _____

Using the information in the chart above, complete the following Venn diagram:

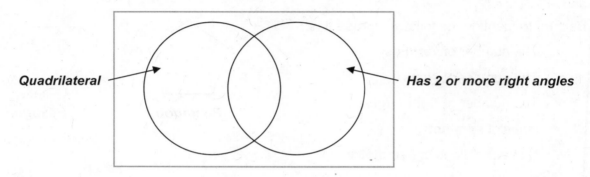

Quadrilateral   Has 2 or more right angles

2. Using figures A through I above, complete the charts and Venn diagrams below.

a)

Property	Figures with this property:
1. Quadrilateral	
2. Equilateral (all sides are the same length)	

Which figures share both properties? _____

Using the information in the chart above, complete the following Venn diagram.

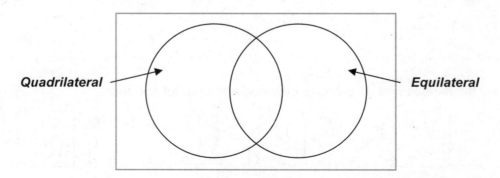

Quadrilateral   Equilateral

b)

Property	Figures with this property:
1. 4 or 5 vertices	
2. 1 or more right angles	

Which figures share both properties? _____

Using the information in the chart above, complete the following Venn diagram.

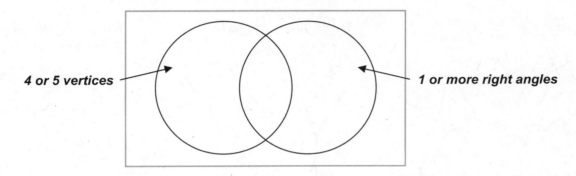

4 or 5 vertices   **1 or more right angles**

3. Below, using two properties of your own, make a Venn diagram as in the questions above.

Properties you might use are:

- Number of vertices
- Lines of symmetry
- Number of right angles
- Number of sides
- Equilateral

Quick Figure Reference Guide *(from the previous page)*

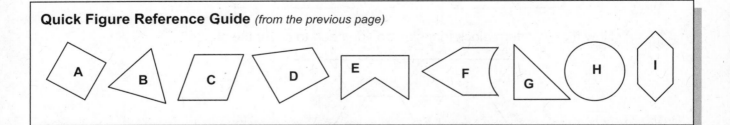

1. Draw …

a) 2 lines to make
   3 congruent squares:

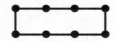

b) 2 lines to make
   3 congruent squares:

c) 2 lines to make
   3 congruent rectangles:

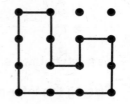

2. These are kites:

These are not kites:

Which of these shapes
is a kite? Explain.

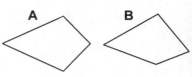

3. Join points A and B with a line. Then join C and D.
   What kind of shapes did you create?

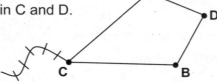

4. Describe any polygons you see in these flags.

a)

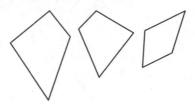

United Kingdom

b)

Trinidad and Tobago

c)

Bahamas

TEACHER: You will need pattern blocks for the following question.

5. a) Make shape **A** with pattern blocks. Can you make shape **B** with the same set of blocks?

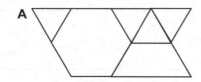   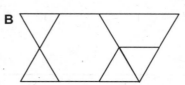

b) How many pattern block triangles do you need to cover the shape?

   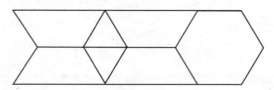

1. Look at the numbered shapes within this figure. Find two shapes that are congruent.

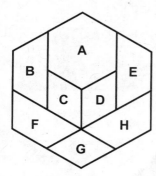

     a) Shapes _____ and _____ are congruent.

     b) How do you know? _____

     _____

     _____

     c) List any other groups of congruent shapes you see.

     _____

     _____

     _____

2. How many <u>triangles</u> are hiding in each of the following figures?
Make copies of the triangle and shade each hidden triangle. (See a) as an example.)

a)

Answer:

This figure contains
__3__ triangles.

b)

This figure contains
____ triangles.

c)

This figure contains
____ triangles.

d)

This figure contains
____ triangles.

e)

This figure contains
____ triangles.

3. How many <u>rectangles</u> are hiding in each of the following figures?
NOTE: A square is a rectangle.

a)

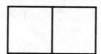

This figure contains ____ rectangles.

b)

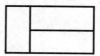

This figure contains ____ rectangles.

G3-17: Puzzles and Problems *(continued)*

4. Circle the shapes that can be <u>folded</u> into matching halves. For each, draw in **all** appropriate lines of symmetry using a ruler. (One shape has multiple lines of symmetry. Can you find it?)

a)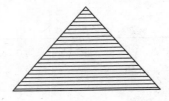

b)

c)

d)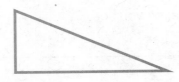

e)

f)

5. How many <u>non-congruent squares</u> can you draw using the grids below?
   HINT: Can you find all five?

   1   2   3   4   5

   I can make ☐ non-congruent (different-sized) squares.

6. What polygons do you see …

   a) in this quilt?

   b) in this rug?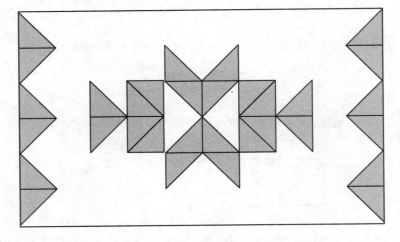

7. Find examples of polygons in your classroom, house, or in books and magazines.

Geometry 1